A DINOSAUR IN WHITEHALL

THE TRUE COST OF DEFENCE PROCUREMENT BUREAUCRACY

Also from Brassey's:

ALLSOP/POPELINSKY
Brassey's Essential Guide to Military Small Arms

BRASSEY'S/CENTRE FOR DEFENCE STUDIES
Brassey's Defence Yearbook 1997

DE WIJK
NATO on the Brink of the New Millennium

SHEFFIELD (ED)
Leadership and Command: The Anglo-American Military Experience since 1861

Brig Bill Kincaid CBE

Brigadier John William 'Bill' Martin Kincaid died suddenly on 21 September aged 76, leaving behind his wife Hilary and three children, John, Charlie and Rebecca. He was the son of Major John Kincaid RA who, as BMRA of the 6th Airborne Division, was killed during Operation Varsity, the crossing of the Rhine in March 1945.

Educated at Cheltenham College, Bill was commissioned from Sandhurst into the Gunners in 1961. He read engineering at Fitzwilliam College, Cambridge from where he gained a BA and later an MA. Regimental duty included tours in 3 RHA in Detmold; 18 Fd Regt in Munsterlager and Hong Kong; and 16 Lt AD Regt in Barton Stacey and Soest, including an emergency tour in Northern Ireland. The Staff College at Shrivenham and Camberley was followed by the first of many tours in the MOD. He commanded 76 (Maude's) Bty, a

2016

CBE for his outstanding contribution to Defence: he was also awarded the Lefroy Gold Medal for "furthering the science and application of artillery."

During this time in MOD Bill developed and expressed deeply held critical views about the many weaknesses in the MOD procurement system: critical but also constructive as he was convinced that things could and should be done better. In retirement he published a series of four books all of which had "Dinosaur" in the title, which explored how procurement processes could be improved, to

These listings are derived from information provided by APC and the *London Gazette*. They have been checked for accuracy of reproduction. Accuracy of information itself

Lt	SJ	Geering	HQ 12 Armd Bde	SO3 G2	Apr 17
Lt	BJ	Rogers	ANAOA	Pl Comd	Mar 17
Lt	JP	Tooze	HQ 38 Irish Bde	SO3 Wtkpr	Nov 16
Lt	J	Wade	CBFSAI	ADC	Apr 17

Promotions

To Lieutenant Colonel

Maj	TN	Mason
Maj	KD	Radwell
Maj	A	Edwards
Maj	JJ	Potter
Maj	AM	Wood
Maj	DK	Smith
Maj	SCD	Culver
Maj	RD	Evans

To Warrant Officer Class Two

WO2	SN	Denby	19 Regt RA
WO2	C	Glover	DAC
WO2	M	Richards	3 RHA
WO2	B	Thomson	19 Regt RA
WO2	AW	Varney	47 Regt RA

To Staff Sergeant

SSgt	AT	Boddy	26 Regt RA
SSgt	SP	Byrne	3 RHA
SSgt	MJ	Chaddock	47 Regt RA

LBdr	RJ	Copley	4 Regt RA
LBdr	IC	Dalton	4 Regt RA
LBdr	R	D'arcy	3 RHA
LBdr	KT	Davies	19 Regt RA
LBdr	CC	Drummond	19 Regt RA
LBdr	E	Dupree	29 Cdo Regt RA
LBdr	W	Farquhar	29 Cdo Regt RA
LBdr	DA	Frost	4 Regt RA
LBdr	CS	Fuller	3 RHA
LBdr	M	George	3 RHA
LBdr	SA	Hewart	19 Regt RA
LBdr	JA	Howlett	4 Regt RA
LBdr	B	Jahateh	19 Regt RA
LBdr	CG	Joyce	4 Regt RA
LBdr	TP	King	1 RHA
LBdr	B	Lilley	29 Cdo Regt RA
LBdr	CJ	Mangan	19 Regt RA
LBdr	JP	McGrath	1 RHA
LBdr	K	Melling	19 Regt RA
LBdr	AJ	Miller	3 RHA
LBdr	TC	Mills	19 Regt RA
LBdr	AV	Nye	19 Regt RA
LBdr	S	Patterson	19 Regt RA
LBdr	DE	Pickles	3 RHA
LBdr	T	Pook	29 Cdo Regt RA
LBdr	DT	Pullen	29 Cdo Regt RA
LBdr	PJ	Renshall	29 Cdo Regt RA
LBdr	NC	Rowlands	4 Regt RA

th the originators.

SSgt RA Leonard 3 RHA
SSgt LJ McIntee 47 Regt RA
SSgt PB Pagan-Skelly AFC Harrogate
SSgt RW Thrift 16 Regt RA

To Bombardier

Bdr MS Balawakula 19 Regt RA
Bdr JA Burgess 3 RHA
Bdr JD Crowther 19 Regt RA
Bdr CM Fountain 32 Regt RA
Bdr AM Gibson 32 Regt RA
Bdr AM Gill 32 Regt RA
Bdr CM Goulding 7 Para RHA
Bdr NP Halden-Evans AFC Harrogate
Bdr L Hollands 19 Regt RA
Bdr K Joubert 19 Regt RA
Bdr CM Makhaye 19 Regt RA
Bdr MR Popejoy 4 Regt RA
Bdr Y Rai 19 Regt RA
Bdr M Szacsky 29 Cdo Regt RA
Bdr J Turner 3 RHA
Bdr DP Vincent 12 Regt RA

To Lance Bombardier

LBdr MJ Anderson 29 Cdo Regt RA
LBdr JPG Barrass 19 Regt RA
LBdr NL Bradley 4 Regt RA
LBdr BPT Bradshaw 1 RHA
LBdr B Brocklehurst 19 Regt RA
LBdr AL Cassel 19 Regt RA
LBdr J Cook 19 Regt RA
LBdr NJ Smith 29 Cdo Regt RA
LBdr SCJ Tabberner 1 RHA
LBdr LA Templeton 29 Cdo Regt RA
LBdr DS Trace 19 Regt RA
LBdr NJ Whitehead 29 Cdo Regt RA
LBdr H Williams 1 RHA
LBdr K Wolecki 3 RHA
LBdr PS Wootton 19 Regt RA

Gazette

REGULAR ARMY

Regular Commissions (Late Entry)

Maj (Acting Lt Col) SP Andrews to be Lt Col 28 August 2016
Lt Col NJ Cole MBE retires 30 August 2016
Maj S Ward retires 28 August 2016

Intermediate Regular Commissions (Late Entry)

Maj DG Wood retires 11 August 2016

Short Service Commissions

Capt AJ Blowers retires 26 August 2016
Lt OJ Davies to be Capt 10 August 2016
Lt WT Hill retires 10 August 2016
Lt BJ Hughes to be Capt 10 August 2016
Lt TPJ Nolan to be Capt 10 August 2016
AG Speechley to be Lt (on probation) 30 August 2016 with seniority 27 December 2014 (formerly Army Reserve)
Lt S Thompson to be Capt 10 August 2016

and technical bent suited this role perfectly, and his battery sailed over all the hurdles with colours flying".

Bill then embarked on a series of tours in the MOD, in the operational requirements, intelligence and procurement branches, where he gained a reputation as a highly professional, intelligent and forward thinking weapons staff officer, and it was here that he really made his mark. Initially working largely on Gunner equipment projects, it is perhaps not too much to claim that his influence ensured the Gunners had an equipment programme to equal the best in the world. In his last appointment as Director of Operational Requirements (Land) he had OR responsibility for the day-to-day direction of the total land systems programme across equipment for all arms and services. There can have been few officers who so directly affected the MOD acquisition process. Nineteen years as an MOD warrior with only a short interlude at the NDC was a punishing commitment requiring dedication and stamina. In 1995 he was appointed as

into the hands of troops faster. Little did he know that they would become required reading for aspiring weapons staff officers, or that he would be invited to lecture at Shrivenham and the Royal United Services Institute! He set up his own consultancy where he put his vast experience to work advising the MOD, the Defence Evaluation and Research Agency and a wide range of defence companies. He also edited The RUSI Defence Systems Journal.

However, there was much more to the man than this factual account of his career. Bill had many abiding passions, the first of which was his wife and family, closely followed by cricket, opera and ballet, singing, his garden and the Clan Kincaid. He packed more into his life than most people. His cricketing exploits were legendary, playing for and often captaining regimental sides; BAOR; the Gunners of which he became Chairman; Combined Services Hong Kong; the Stragglers of Asia; and the Sunbury Cricket Club where he played regularly for over 40 years. He wrote the definitive history of the SCC on its 75th anniversary.

He developed a passion for opera and ballet while still at school, and it was through that, while at Cambridge, that he met his wife who was herself a ballet dancer. They were regular patrons of Covent Garden and other venues. He sang with the Hong Kong Choral Society, the Whitehall Choir and the Treasury Singers among others. His small garden was packed with a glorious collection of fuchsias, with not a square inch of open space to spare. He carried out exhaustive research into the history of the Clan Kincaid, and published a very readable history under the title of "This I'll Defend," the Clan motto.

Bill Kincaid was a man of many parts with enormous energy and a wide range of interests. He was a force for good in many areas of life, especially in Defence procurement and in cricket. He will be sorely missed by his family, by his many military colleagues and friends and by the world of cricket which he loved, remaining a passionate vice-president of Gunner cricket right up to the end of his life.

A DINOSAUR IN WHITEHALL

THE TRUE COST OF DEFENCE PROCUREMENT BUREAUCRACY

Bill Kincaid

*with cartoons by **Jim Potts***

BRASSEY'S
London * Washington

First English Edition 1997

UK editorial offices: Brassey's, 33 John Street, London WC1N 2AT
UK orders: Marston Book Services, PO Box 269, Abingdon, OX14 4SD

North American orders: Brassey's Inc., PO Box 960,
Herndon, VA 22070, USA

Library of Congress Cataloging in Publication Data
Kincaid, Bill.
    A dinosaur in Whitehall: the true cost of defence procurement
bureaucracy/Bill Kincaid: with cartoons by Jim Potts. — 1st
English ed.
        p. cm.
    Includes bibliographical references.
    ISBN 1–85753–257–0 (hardcover)
    1. Great Britain. Ministry of Defence—Procurement.
2. Bureaucracy—Great Britain. I. Title.
UC265.G7K56 1997
355.6'212'0941—dc21   97–25838
                                               CIP

British Library Cataloguing in Publication Data
A catalogue record for this book is available from the British Library

ISBN 1 85753 257 0 Hardcover

Typeset by York House Typographic Ltd, London
Printed in Great Britain by Biddles Short Run Books, King's Lynn, Norfolk

CONTENTS

Few people think more than two or three times a year; I have made an international reputation for myself by thinking once or twice a week.

GEORGE BERNARD SHAW

CHAPTER ONE

A Dinosaur in Whitehall

There are more civilians employed by the Ministry of Defence (MOD) than there are soldiers in the post-Cold War Army.[1] This may come as some surprise, even to fans of such programmes as *Yes, Minister*, but the figures are official. What on earth do all these civilians do? Who are they and are they really necessary? Do they interface with, or overlap, the military officers in MOD? These questions spring to mind readily but there are no clear answers; despite the Options for Change exercise and the more recent Defence Costs Study there has been no clear examination of the overall system of defence management. This would seem to be a major omission: if we devote more effort to the high-level management of the Services than to manning the Army, we must be quite sure that we are getting value for money.

The general view of outsiders is that MOD is a huge, bloated department where everything takes forever, where the most useful day-to-day activity is to stick a few fingers into the disintegrating dyke, and where the officials at the top are out of touch, master-minding major change with their vision impaired almost entirely by irrelevant and preconceived notions. These outsiders may have been conditioned to some extent by TV programmes, newspaper articles and cartoons that see any government department as a fossilised outfit run by classical scholars striving continually to outwit ministers and to block all progress good or bad; but they believe that there is more than a grain or two of truth in such portrayals. Yet outsiders are outsiders and do not have a full view. More pertinent perhaps is that many insiders believe that in some respects at least, life in MOD runs to a more extreme script than any *Yes, Minister* writer or producer would dare to screen lest they provoke incredulity. Are these insiders just tired, old cynics with no further hope of promotion and a vested interest in portraying all those who have got on in their place as incompetents, born with silver spoons in their mouths? Certainly these cynics exist, but in recent years there has been an increasing dissatisfaction with the existing organisations, procedures and practices amongst the most capable, younger

officers. Is this just inexperience or impatience? Or could it be insight?

The recent extensive changes in world politics and the implications for the defence budget have of course caused turmoil amongst career officers. Many have had to think about the future seriously for the first time and could no longer take for granted a guaranteed full career to the age of 55. Of course thinking is not always welcomed, particularly not by those with closed minds. Such people do not think and they are uncomfortable with those who do, preferring to follow blindly existing procedures and practices. After all they might be asked why this and why not the other. Of course nobody will admit to having a closed mind, and everybody claims to welcome radical thinking – always provided that such thinking attacks other people's sacred cows rather than their own.

As Shakespeare put it, through the mouth of Julius Caesar,

Yond Cassius has a lean and hungry look / He thinks too much / Such men are dangerous.

Thinking is dangerous and is done much more comfortably in a committee where no-one is fully responsible and blame cannot be made to stick. MOD is the home of the committee. Someone (to my regret I no longer remember who) once said: 'One of the generally amiable idiosyncrasies of man is his ability to expend a great deal of effort without much enquiry as to the end result.' He was commenting on the human race in general. MOD is staffed by human beings and this 'generally amiable idiosyncrasy' is alive and well. Indeed, outside MOD the military often display the same characteristic and believe it better to run hard in any direction than to walk slowly towards the destination. Action is often confused with progress: in MOD, inaction is also often confused with progress.

In 1982, Brian Taylor, a senior civil servant, wrote that the 'MOD is in trimmer shape physically, no longer a bureaucratic Billy Bunter'.[2] This suggests that in 1982 there was an official view that for many years MOD had been a bureaucratic Billy Bunter. I believe there is a widespread view that during the days of a buoyant defence budget, growing at 3 per cent per year in real terms, there was enormous fat in MOD. To believe that it is no longer a bureaucratic Billy Bunter is not necessarily a viewpoint that will be echoed in the early years of the next century. Certainly there has been action, but we must not mistake action for progress. The question concerns the amount of progress that may have been made.

There has indeed been action and this has led to a considerable amount of slimming down, improved efficiency, rationalisation, hiving off to the private sector and other good cries. My own studies, admittedly rather superficial, have shown that in one small area of the MOD equipment world, workload per head has increased by 400 per cent. This looks good. However, if you measured a horse's potential performance by past workload alone, irrespective of the racing conditions and the number and size of the jumps, you are not likely to win much at the betting shop. In MOD during this increase in workload the obstacles have proliferated and have become larger, so that in terms of useful output per head progress is much less.

I used to think that MOD was good at making minor decisions slowly, but I am not sure now that I was right. It is incontrovertible that big decisions take a mighty long time. For example, the 'tank decision' to select a new tank to replace the Royal Armoured Corps' ageing Chieftains took seven years, not including the time taken before to assemble most of the data. Yes, seven years for one decision.

Of course big decisions with many complicated and serious implications cannot be taken overnight. There is an overriding need to protect the taxpayers' money from waste. This means that risks must be minimised and that all sensible options must be examined properly, and this takes time. However, in all walks of business, time is money and the longer the decision takes, the more the equipment costs in due course. This is obvious, as industry cannot sit around for nothing: the work force still has to be paid, and design teams have to be kept together and available. If time is indeed money, a balance must be found between decision-making time and risk acceptance. Only in this way will the taxpayer be given real value for money. The big question here is whether we have got this balance right.

Decision-making time needs some amplification. The seven years of the tank decision were due to procrastination at the top level over which tank to buy. In reality, there is a continuous stream of decisions that have to be made at all levels, but particularly at the lowest technical levels. Hold-ups here, though they may be measured only in months, weeks or days, will add up to enormous periods because there are so many of them. Again there must be a balance between time for consideration and the cost of that time. Decisions, once made, are often irreversible or at the very best costly to change. They must be right. This leads to the argument that all decisions, except the most straightforward, need to be referred upwards and sideways to ensure that all aspects have been considered properly. But this is very time-consuming.

Scrutiny is obviously necessary to a certain degree. Without it, the risks of future Nimrods will increase; without it, the invitation to fraud is extensive. But just how much scrutiny and how often is the point at issue. If you line up ten full-time accountants, consumer experts and investment gurus, you might expect your household costs to drop and your savings to multiply. But does it make sense to spend so much money on reducing risk in your budget?

Whatever level of scrutiny is built in it must work or it is a waste of time, effort and, above all, money. Does the extensive scrutiny in MOD work? If it does not, it must be changed radically; if it does, could it work as well or at least to an adequate level with markedly less effort? Just how often does all this scrutiny lead to the reversal of a proposal made originally at working level? Or even to a modification?

These questions are vital, yet they do not seem to have been considered at all at high level within MOD. They are vital because of the sheer size of the sums of money involved. Equipment procurement costs around £9bn per year for the three Services, more than the total cost of manning, maintaining and operating the whole Army. A significant improvement in procurement efficiency would release large sums of money for the Services or, alternatively, to buy more and better equipment for the same cost. A worthy goal, surely? But can we improve efficiency without risk escalating to an unacceptable degree?

A 1995 MOD study described the views of defence suppliers as follows:

> *MOD is perceived to be a bureaucratic dinosaur ... mountains of documentation ... endless committees ... difficulties in establishing where the buck stops ... slow decision making ... not organised for effective management.* [3]

This is pretty damning – but defence suppliers would say that, wouldn't they? More convincing perhaps is the finding of the Defence Costs Study of the need 'to tackle the common complaint at all levels that the committee culture is seen as leading to lack of decision and poor compromise solutions'.

Bureaucracy is defined as a 'system of administration based upon a hierarchy of authority etc.'.[4] That in itself should not give it a bad name. But it has become tainted in use and the same dictionary defines a bureaucrat as 'an official who adheres to bureaucracy esp. rigidly'. Here again is the suggestion of a lack of thinking and a reliance on tired old procedures.

MOD is of course one of the big spending ministries, and the bigger the expenditure the more efficient it should be. A friend of mine, a senior official in the Department of the Environment, believes that rigid bureaucracy in MOD is worse than in other government departments, with more people involved in decision-making and more vested interests apparent. Certainly, military officers arriving for the first time for a tour of duty in MOD are almost without exception badly depressed by the slow pace of progress and the height of the bureaucratic hurdles. Outside views are not always correct, nor are first impressions of insiders, but taken together they suggest that there is considerable feeling that all is not well. This should be taken seriously.

MOD seems to be unique amongst ministries in employing very large numbers of its 'customers' at all levels. This ought to be a major strength. There is a clash of cultures between the military action men and civil servant caution but each has undoubted strengths and weaknesses. The military officer will bring a sense of urgency, a wealth of field experience and an ability to balance factors to achieve a satisfactory end result. He may not be quite so interested in financial approval limits or political sensitivities, but here the civil servant can apply his particular strengths. However, the civil servant will be happy to delay while bureaucratic i's are dotted and t's crossed; delay will also come naturally to the scientist who will be primarily interested in technological options, the best of which are likely to be less mature and therefore further in the future. It is then up to the military officer to refocus all their eyes on the need to meet a particular deployment date. Working together, the military officer, the civil servant and the scientist can be a strong team. This does happen, but regrettably too seldom. Too often, individuals retreat into a laager mentality and all sympathetic contact is lost. Combining their strengths should be a major advantage, yet too often it appears as if it is policy to set them against each other.

Far more attention has been given to combining the three Services and to eliminating inter-Service strife. A fully 'purple' staff has been seen as the eventual goal by many people since Mountbatten took the first steps down this road. Michael Heseltine took it further, but this left the Services sitting uncomfortably between the two stools of single-Service and fully 'purple' staff, with more overheads yet little real progress. In the Defence Costs Study, a little more progress was made towards the goal of the 'purple' stool but not much of it benefited procurement. If and when that stool is reached, will it make much difference, or will it be seen as a side issue? Is not the co-operation of civil servants and the military far more important? Or is this not the real issue either?

The people issue is inevitably central. Any large organisation depends on the people who run it and the people who work for it. Quality counts. Procedures can, given the will, be changed overnight; people cannot, at least not in large numbers. But quality on its own is insufficient; attitude is important, too. Attitude means, amongst other things, the confidence to investigate objectively and to take hard decisions at the right time. While most, some perhaps grudgingly, would agree that there is considerable quality in both the military and the Civil Service, almost all would question the attitudes in MOD. Is this fair?

There is an old joke about the lion that broke out of London Zoo early one Sunday morning and after wandering about found itself in Whitehall. It broke into MOD and made a lair in an office. It survived by eating one civil servant a day. No-one noticed. The lion then made a fatal mistake and ate one of the catering staff, whereupon it was discovered, captured and taken back to the zoo. This joke survives because MOD is widely seen as a slumbering giant where the real world goes unnoticed. As recent changes in the world have been so great, the slumbering giant has now woken and has been seen to flex his muscles. The parallels with Richard Wagner's opera *Siegfried* are disturbing: the giant Fafner turns himself into a dragon to guard his treasure, over which he slumbers; when awoken, he is killed by the hero Siegfried who takes possession of the loot. For Fafner read MOD, for Siegfried read the Treasury. But this is not all. Many people have been quick to point out that it is not a giant or a dragon that has been disturbed, but a dinosaur.

A dinosaur in Whitehall is a serious charge indeed. This book will examine that charge, but it will concentrate on one area only: that of equipment procurement with its expenditure of £9bn per year. Of course, to do this it will have to look wider than just at the part of MOD dealing with equipment: it will have to examine all parts that affect the way procurement is carried out. In the first part I will look at the people, the procedures and the decision-making process, at efficiency and at the vital safeguards for the taxpayer. I will identify the major weaknesses that reduce performance and efficiency. Much of this will seem very contentious, but only to those who have not thought about these matters clearly before. Of course it is easy to criticise, less easy to identify options for improving the system and the obstacles that will have to be overcome. The second part of this book will do just this.

In other words I will attempt to answer two questions: Is a dinosaur at large in Whitehall? And if so, how can we convert it into a Rolls Royce carrying an integrated crew of a scientist driver, a military map-reader and a civil servant in charge of the petrol coupons, all working in harmony?

PART ONE
THE PROBLEMS

CHAPTER TWO
The Military

Prejudice against innovation, a typical characteristic of an Officer Corps which has grown up in a well tried and proven system.
FIELD MARSHAL ERWIN ROMMEL

There is no doubt that the stock of the British armed forces stands high in public esteem, both national and international. Indeed, the 1994 *Statement on the Defence Estimates*, in one of its few wholly unambiguous and fully truthful passages, has the following to say:

> *The United Kingdom remains one of the world's most formidable powers ... the armed forces of the United Kingdom who, in terms of their experience, training and esprit, are a match for any in the world ... our armed forces are widely regarded – and rightly – as a valuable and prestigious national asset.*[1]

Not many would challenge this, even if there are many aspects which could and should be improved, some of them drastically and urgently. Nevertheless the Services are in good shape, with an officer corps widely regarded as professional, capable and highly principled. Why then should Alan Clark, in his diaries, rail against top Army officers as follows:

> *I want to fire the whole lot. Instantly. Out, out. No 'District' commands, no golden bowlers, nothing. Out. There are so many good, tough, keen young officers who aren't full of shit. How can we bring them on, before they get disillusioned or conventionalised by the system?*[2]

Can a highly effective Army really be regarded as a 'valuable and prestigious national asset' if it is peopled at the highest level by officers 'full of shit'? Do we need to take Clark seriously, or is it one of his typical throwaway, tongue-in-cheek statements designed to provoke?

Clark on his own could perhaps be dismissed as an eccentric and without other serious indications there would be no real case to answer. But there is other evidence, although much of it is subjective opinion often based on considerable ignorance. This evidence, like Clark's, only makes a partial case; it shows quite clearly that unlike the high ability of the field commanders and their senior staff in military headquarters, the performance of some senior officers in MOD is of a far lower standard, at times bordering on the inadequate, at least in crucial parts of their jobs. This perception of inadequacy is pretty widespread amongst a large number of more junior but most capable officers serving in MOD today. It has been apparent for at least the last decade, but I do not believe it has been held so widely and deeply as it is today – in the aftermath of the perceived failing of top military management during years of unprecedented change, begun by the fall of Communism, and the slashing of the defence budget in the over-hasty chase of a 'defence dividend'. In actual fact, changes were bound to occur after a period of Cold War stagnation once the major increases in defence spending over the early 1980s tailed off. Nevertheless, the changes that have occurred have been far greater than anyone would have considered possible in 1989. However hard the task of managing such change, the widespread in-house military perception is that numbers of senior officers in MOD have failed the Army. It is irrelevant to ask how many of these critics could have done better; far more relevant is the question whether anyone else might have done better, given the difficulties of the Whitehall system itself. Is it the prejudice against innovation that Rommel observed, as quoted at the head of this chapter, or is it an inability to think?

The general perception is that many of the most senior officers are, and have been for some time, ineffective; that they appear old, a little decrepit, self-satisfied, with nowhere to go next except retirement. They are all typically between 50 and 65 years old and, perhaps unsurprisingly, seem to be running out of steam. They appear to be happier discussing regimental titles, bands and uniforms rather than military concepts, doctrine or equipment.

There are clearly exceptions to this perception of inadequacy – Generals Sir Hugh Beach and Sir Richard (now Field Marshal the Lord) Vincent were brilliant Masters General of the Ordnance, and several others were or still are effective, knowledgeable and intelligent, but the general view is that the senior officers are largely ineffective. There is a good reason for this: the real lack of power and influence the system gives these military men in some areas, most notably the equipment programme. I shall return to this in a later chapter.

But this cannot be a complete defence. More pertinent is the question of whether the right men are in the right top jobs. The Army's promotion system is built on ability in field command. A brilliant peacetime commander who is a hopeless staff officer can reach the top; conversely a less able commander will be unlikely to progress beyond the middle ranks whatever his brilliance as a staff officer. The qualities that make a good commander in the field, however – the ability to make swift, sound decisions, to give clear orders, to see they are carried out to a high standard, to motivate – are not those which are in the greatest demand in MOD jobs, where diplomacy, persuasion, understanding of complex problems and procedures, and 'the art of the practical' are more important. The poor military officer has to work with civil servants, for heaven's sake! It is rare in any walk of life for one person to combine such a wide array of talents and it is even less likely to occur in somebody who has spent most of his life commanding or supporting a commander in a field formation. The translation from field to Ministry is a major step. Are there parallels in other walks of life? Scientists do sometimes move from research to management, although most do not make this move and many of those who do fail completely.

An Army officer's move to a top job in MOD is therefore a very difficult step. Many cannot cope but get out of office as often as they can to 'talk to the chaps' in Cyprus, Hong Kong, Belize or anywhere. Whitehall business is given short shrift and major issues go by the board. As civil servants are always there, military input to decision-making is often unbalanced.

In an article on officer career structures for top Army appointments in the *British Army Review*, Major Ashbrooke sums up the qualities required extremely well:

> *Command requires certain skills and a certain psychological temperament, particularly in war. Different staff jobs require different abilities. Some require very creative minds. For others a very good memory is an asset. The ability to think on one's feet and to debate issues is an asset in some areas. Self discipline and the ability to write are a great advantage in some but not all appointments. Most senior officers will have some of these abilities; very few, if any, will have all.*[3]

He goes on to analyse the top jobs in the Army and shows that few are genuine command posts; yet the Army promotion system will select good field commanders for all top jobs regardless of their other qualities. It is hardly surprising then that many incumbents are ill-suited to the posts they hold. Of the 19 jobs he analysed, only six were genuine command posts and three of these have since disappeared, while all of the other 13 non-command senior posts remain, 11 of them in MOD (although some, being tri-Service, are not held by generals all the time).

Capability is one aspect, expertise very much another. Is it wise to select top officers with little regard for the qualities they will bring to their jobs? Even if it is, should these officers not have considerable relevant expertise? Ashbrooke goes on to show that

> *With one exception (a logistic corps officer) the post of Quartermaster General in recent years has generally been held by an officer who has had one logistic appointment prior to taking up post. Some have had none ... Most holders of the post of Adjutant General have had no more than one specialist job in the 'A' area prior to taking up post and the average number of 'A' posts is between 1 and 2 ... The last*

Army holder of the post of Chief of Defence Intelligence had never served in an intelligence staff post prior to taking up his appointment.[4]

To this list we could add that most recent holders of the key equipment appointment of Master General of the Ordnance had never served in the Procurement Executive before becoming the top Army man, some of them not having served at all in any related weapons area.

The promotion and selection system therefore seems to be placing an enormously unfair ball and chain on the ability of senior officers to discharge their responsibilities effectively. While it may be a good thing occasionally to introduce a relative outsider, it does not strike me as very sensible to select people with no expertise time after time. Would industry repeatedly select software managers from managers with financial or contractual expertise only? Or would the Metropolitan Police habitually be headed by officers who had only served in Cornwall or the north of Scotland? It takes time to climb the learning curve. At the lowest levels in MOD, it is generally reckoned that majors take about six months to approach full effectiveness in their job; how much longer is it likely to take senior officers with an immensely wider span to discharge their full responsibilities effectively? One year, two, or three? They are only in post for two to three years! Senior officers will therefore rely heavily on their staff for the expertise and history of issues that they lack themselves. But all too often, for the same reasons, the staff lacks both the necessary capabilities and expertise. This is a perfect recipe for reinventing the wheel every three years or so.

Does it matter? The late Admiral of the Fleet, Sir John Fieldhouse, after three years as Chief of the Naval Staff and three years as Chief of the Defence Staff, is quoted as saying: 'I am beginning to find out about battling for resources near the end of the job.' Beginning to learn, after six years, to battle with senior civil servants who have been learning the game for perhaps 40 years and who change the rules as soon as someone like Fieldhouse begins to learn the ropes?

Selection for top jobs should be based on qualities and expertise. Promotion policy must ensure that officers with the right qualities and expertise are available at the highest level. This needs some really creative attention; at the moment, we have got it badly wrong.

The Army is not alone in this as much the same criticism applies to the Royal Navy and the Royal Air Force. But the Army has two further problems all of its own. The first is the Army officers' attitude to equipment. It may be a platitude to say that, while the Navy and the RAF man their equipment, the Army equips the man, but it is true nevertheless. Parliament places a manpower ceiling on the Army, but a ceiling on numbers of surface ships and frontline aircraft squadrons on the Navy and the RAF. Attitudes go with this distinction. How many commanding officers, even in today's highly technical Army, are as interested in the maintenance, care and tactical use of their equipment as they are in the character building and promotion opportunities of their officers and NCOs, in the in-barracks administration of the regiment, or in links with the local community? There are few. In this, of course, they are following the brigade or divisional commander's priorities; but equipment matters are too often left to the 'tradesmen'. When the workshop commander complains about the poor state of equipment maintenance he may be accorded a polite ear but often little more, at least over a sustained period.

The Gulf War is a significant illustration. Fortunately there was a long build-up time as the Army had to find equipment that worked and had to cannibalise remaining equipment to provide a level of spares far above that officially provisioned; once the operation had been completed brilliantly, equipment was often left uncared for. This is of course nothing new. Recruits, particularly officer recruits, do not join the Army to operate equipment or to supervise maintenance, they join for other reasons. In days gone by they joined for the horses and it was a major disappointment when the Army became mechanised. The Army only reluctantly accepted mechanisation. Earl Haig said in 1921:

I am certainly not among those who hold that the place of flesh and blood, in man and horse, can ever be wholly taken by petrol and machinery ... Tanks and aeroplanes and heavy guns ... have not yet served to eliminate the horse which ... is a part of the man himself.[5]

The cavalry changed their allegiance from the horse to the tank only reluctantly and generations later, having learned to live with the tank, showed no interest in the helicopter. And yet 'air cavalry' is a logical addition to the armoured corps and, if made, would have saved many historical regiments which have since disappeared.

This disregard for, and often complete ignorance of, equipment is widespread and clearly visible amongst staff officers in MOD. We have precious little Army equipment doctrine and equipment matters, however serious, are pushed off hastily to the 'specialists'. Not so long ago when a lot of equipment in the British Army on the Rhine was showing appallingly low reliability, senior officers and ministers would return to MOD after visits to Germany demanding action from equipment procurement branches which had no responsibility whatever for in-Service equipment. Much of the problem lay in poor equipment maintenance in the units, insufficient training and undermanning in the repair chain and, as such, was very much a command problem; nevertheless general after general shuffled this off as equipment failure and the province of the 'specialists'.

I well remember the saga of the air defence gun. In the late 1970s the Soviet armed helicopter threat became ominously clear and a decision was made to provide extra funding for an Army air defence weapon to supplement the all-missile defence provided by Rapier and Blowpipe. 'We must have an air defence gun', said the generals and may well have added in their minds, 'something that goes bang at both ends'. However, fairly soon the scientific and military studies began to show that a small missile system was far more cost-effective than any gun system. The generals were seduced by the Soviet ZSU-23-4 and the US 'Sgt. York'. But what is suitable for a huge superpower which can deploy thousands of guns is not necessarily suitable for a smaller power which could only deploy tens. It was not long before 'Sgt. York' bit the dust in disgrace after a VIP demonstration in which it apparently refused to engage the helicopter targets and insisted on shooting up the VIP lavatory – which it did with devastating effect. But such amusement was still in the future, and the generals wanted a gun. Their staffs refused to pass on the bad news coming out of the studies, which incidentally were extremely well done and remain robust to criticism to this day. I was told to explain the facts of life to the generals. Most were quick to appreciate the situation and support a missile solution, although some did so more graciously than others. But one of them was prepared to die in the proverbial ditch marked 'gun'. In the end only a high-level 'package' brought him on board. Today the winner of the competition, the Short's HVM system, is in Service and looks a world-beater.

The lack of equipment knowledge is clear in many places. When I was selected for promotion from lieutenant colonel to colonel, I was asked by the postings organisation at Stanmore what I wanted to do. I replied that I wanted to remain in the weapons field, primarily in the artillery or air defence disciplines, and that I preferred to work in Central London so that I could commute daily from my own home. I was well aware how difficult a job it was to fit square pegs in square holes all the time – those involved lost no opportunity in telling me so – but I was a little surprised to find myself being run for a job at the Chemical and Biological Defence Establishment at Porton Down near Salisbury. I could not detect even the semblance of a square hole – not rectangular, not even octagonal, it seemed wholly round. Stanmore just did not understand. It was technical, wasn't it? Not in London, of course, but otherwise pretty near to what I wanted. After some high-level lobbying the suggestion got knocked on the head. I next found that I was being run for a job at what was then called the Royal Armament Research and Development Establishment (RARDE) at Fort Halstead in Kent. This was a little nearer the mark but it was hardly a daily commute from Walton-on-Thames in Surrey. Stanmore was exasperated when I failed to jump over the moon, but it turned out that in their complete ignorance of the technical world – in contrast they would have a detailed knowledge of every non-technical post in the whole Army – they believed that RARDE was located not in Kent but at St Christopher House in Southwark. Easy enough to make such a mistake if you have no idea what the posts entail, but surely it is not difficult to envisage the difficulties associated with carrying out anti-tank missile warhead research in the middle of South London.

Alas, this is not an isolated instance. A senior officer asked me if I thought that the post of Master General of the Ordnance was really necessary as he was doing a study to recommend reduction of top posts. I found this rather odd and wondered why he thought MGO was less important than others. Well, you know, it's only a part-time post and rather peripheral to matters of moment, he said. A few more remarks and the penny dropped. He was confusing MGO with the Master Gunner of St James's Park!

Yet another senior officer, an equipment director, was convinced that his personal direct line to the Commander-in-Chief of the British Army of the Rhine was all-conquering and that the underlings in MOD, such as the Master General of the Ordnance and the Assistant Chief of the Defence Staff (Operational Requirements), who in reality are the true powers, were of no account and could be ignored. Still another swore to me that in the end I would 'do what the Director Royal Artillery tells you', despite my patient explanations that I worked for an admiral of higher rank and that I would do as he ordered!

Ignorance of equipment procurement is therefore widespread, especially at high level. Some will claim that things are improving as more and more officers have technical training, but I cannot detect any increase in absolute equipment interest, particularly once a new weapon is in Service. Certainly amongst the brigadiers I have lately been dealing with, most of them in their late 40s, very few show any interest in equipment matters generally or even in specific and important issues relating to them. They are just not enthused.

The other problem is that central glory of the Army, the regimental system. Without doubt it has contributed enormously in the past, and perhaps still does today, to the morale and motivation of individual soldiers, small teams, companies, squadrons, batteries, battalions and regiments. In peace it gives a sense of belonging, in war a higher motivation. Whether its advantages are quite as great as many of its proponents claim I am not so sure, but it would be a foolhardy person who claims there are none. Rightly or wrongly, the retention of the regimental system was laid down as the prime *sine qua non* at the start of deliberations on the future structure of the smaller army under Options for Change in the wake of the disintegration of Communism in 1990 and 1991.

The regimental system does, however, cause problems in MOD. While the Navy and the RAF are able to come fairly easily to Service decisions, this is not the case within the Army. A senior Army officer cannot just forget his background, for that background will have conditioned, for example, a former Royal Armoured Corps officer to know – not to think, to know – that tanks make much more sense than anything else. This conditioning makes it difficult for him to appreciate arguments relating to other capability areas. The same goes for infantrymen and, to a lesser extent, for gunners and sappers. Scratch any officer in a non-regimental post and you will see the cap-badge; the bigger the issue, the clearer it shines. Perhaps this is inevitable but it does not help the Army in their tussles with the other two Services.

The RAF has a clear single-Service view on everything and all its officers in single and central staff posts hold to that line whatever the tri-Service arguments – there is no such thing as a 'purple' RAF officer; the Royal Navy hold themselves to be senior, superior and above all; the Army squabble among their cap-badges, making it easy for others to fight what is clearly a far from robust Army position. The other Services and the civil servants in particular cash in quite easily.

Not that the civil servants need much help anyway. More intelligent, more experienced, more knowledgeable, less principled, without clear responsibility except to balance the books, they can take the military to the cleaners whenever they like. Nevertheless, the military help them by shooting themselves in the foot time and again. How can civilians accept statements about the pain of a savings measure when there are so many instances of waste elsewhere? Many examples have been splashed across the papers in recent times. It hardly helps if, when accused of using defence funds for fox-hunting, the Army spokesman explains that it is necessary to have riding skills for ceremonial duties. More worrying still is the recent publicity over the cost of houses and the scale of house staff for senior officers. Some are ludicrously over the top, and there is a reluctance to acknowledge that we are to some extent living in the past. There is of course a clear necessity for certain senior officers to live in reasonably prestigious houses and to entertain officially on a fairly frequent basis, and this should be made crystal clear to the media. But there is no doubt that the frequency of entertaining is far more than is really justified in today's modern and smaller Army. Visits by foreign generals or by senior officers or officials in Britain, if the distance is large, call for some quality hospitality. But how necessary is much of it, or is it just nice to have old friends to stay? Whatever the answer, there is enough evidence of unnecessary expenditure to undermine those fighting for funds, or against cuts, in MOD. And how much harm does it do when civilians see the line of large staff cars sitting in the Main Building car park all day waiting to transport one Army Board member back to his flat a few minutes away? Is this really a priority?

The Army rightly prides itself on the complete integrity of its officer corps. There are lapses, of course, but by and large Army officers have high standards of morality and high principles. This is in stark contrast to much of the country: not just politicians, artists and sportsmen but the vast bulk of the nation where adultery, absenteeism and self-profit is rife. Even civil servants, as we shall see in the next chapter, suffer badly in comparison. There is much debate in the Army as to whether this difference in morality distances the Army from the majority of the population to the detriment of recruiting, image and understanding, or whether it actually enhances its appeal. This is not the place for a lengthy investigation of national morality, but the recent publicity over 'Captain Crumpet', the attractive Army officer who dumped her officer husband for a married grenadier guard NCO, showed uncertainty in the media over how to deal with this subject. The *Sun*, of course, applied the sexual angle, but there was curiously little criticism over stuffy Army morals and even less when 'Captain Crumpet Mark Two' appeared later in the year. It seems to me that the country expects Army officers to have high personal and collective standards and to take action to maintain them. The immediate resignation of the Chief of the Defence Staff, Sir Peter Harding, was in clear contrast to the repeated non-resignations of politicians until pressure got too intense. But there is a temptation to which many Army officers fall, and that is an unthinking devotion to 'tradition' and the 'old standards'. There appears to be a reluctance amongst many to try to distinguish between what is of timeless importance and what is mere fashion. This may be difficult but it does not excuse the effort. I am sure that as a brand new second lieutenant in my first battery I made many mistakes, some of them serious. But the most serious according to the adjutant was that I was spotted in the local town one Saturday afternoon in civilian clothes – without a hat. I copped it badly for that.

So what do we make of the senior military officers in MOD? They are loyal, principled, with high standards of behaviour. In most cases they have proved themselves to have sterling qualities of leadership. They are dedicated to doing their best with unstinting effort. They have a fine sense of urgency and of priorities. Against this, however, must be set the fact that by and large they have the wrong qualities for the posts they hold, and lack experience and expertise in most aspects of their posts so that they are no match at all for the wily civil servant. Army officers have two further disadvantages: the regimental system gives them divided loyalties and a less than objective view of matters across the board, and equipment is foreign to their natures and is pushed off onto the specialists. All this plays to the strengths of the civil servants, and now is the moment to look at their place and performance in Whitehall.

CHAPTER THREE

The Civil Servants

I reflected how fortunate it was that thirty years of training in the Civil Service methods had triumphed over my initial impetuosity. So long as there is anything to be gained by saying nothing, it is always better to say nothing than anything.

SIR HUMPHREY APPLEBY, YES, PRIME MINISTER[1]

In the debate on the Defence White Paper in the House of Lords in July 1993, Lord Bramall, as one-time Chief of Defence Staff and President of MCC clearly a pillar of the establishment, said:

> *White Papers, however good, are often just as significant for what they do not say as for what they do ... Certain issues have been fudged ... a certain sleight of hand ... that is having your cake and eating it ... What is particularly galling is when the whole of our defence effort is represented as a perfectly measured response and in the very best interests of the defence of the realm ... power has swung disproportionately to the accountants ... there is a real risk that we will not only get the Armed Forces that the Treasury are prepared to pay for but those in size and shape which the Treasury, in its wisdom, thinks is appropriate.[2]*

Of course he said much more on the ability of the armed forces to sustain an operational capability. The thrust of his remarks was aimed not so much at the politicians, although they carry the ultimate responsibility, but at the civil servants, particularly the financiers who effectively make ministers' policy. Lord Bramall was rightly concerned that it is no longer the Services that make crucial decisions on capability but the financial scrutineers in the Civil Service, particularly those in the Treasury and their henchmen in MOD. This is borne out quite clearly in his closing sentences:

> *Civil servants working primarily in the interests of expediency and balancing the books must not be allowed to take over completely from the doers. Otherwise we are storing up for ourselves dire trouble in an uncertain future.*

The decision-making process in MOD will be examined in a later chapter. In this chapter, it is the civil servants themselves who are under the microscope, much as the military were examined in the last. After I had delivered a lecture to the Army

Command and Staff Course in January 1994 it was suggested that I did not like civil servants, but the listener had mistaken my fairly outspoken attack on the decision-making system and the part civil servants play in it for a personal attack on the civil servants themselves. I clearly made an erroneous impression for I do have a high regard for many of them. As I wrote in the previous chapter, they are in general intelligent, experienced and knowledgeable. Many have first-class degrees (not all in the classical subjects so beloved of Sir Humphrey Appleby, although I have to admit that a minimal classical education is useful when solving *The Times* crossword); many are also most charming companions.

That we have the best Civil Service in the world is a fairly common claim. It may well be true. Nicholas Soames, then Armed Forces Minister, said: 'It is a priceless asset to this country – there's not a shadow of doubt about it.'[3] He criticised the media for portraying stereotypes that perpetuate the general negative perception of the Civil Service and reinforce the views of the general public that it is just a heavyweight bureaucracy filled with time-serving, self-serving people. He said he found it sad that 'loyal, dedicated, clever and able men and women should feel themselves devalued ... I have always been deeply impressed with the officials I have had dealings with.' Clever and able – certainly. Loyal and dedicated – yes, but to what? Sir Colin Southgate, the businessman who headed the 1994 review of the Treasury, said that the only valuable asset of the Treasury was its people, who needed to be trained, developed, supported and managed better. These talented and committed people deeply believed in public Service. The problem since the war has been in his opinion that Britain has found it so difficult to channel those qualities.[4]

If the average civil servant is far more intelligent than the average military officer – and the gap is closing – he is a lot less principled, and here I am not sure the gap is closing at all. Although the youth of this country is reported to have increasing difficulty in distinguishing right from wrong, if you were to ask the man in the No 88 'Clapham Omnibus' if he knew what truth is, he would probably say yes – at least he would claim to know when he had stated an untruth. That is not to say he will necessarily always tell the truth, or even try and minimise the untruth he tells. Most of those avoiding the truth are well aware that they are doing so; it is not a complicated subject. This is equally true for the military. Truth is a fundamentally straightforward concept. What, then, are we to make of the following: 'Truth is a very difficult concept, many faceted.'[5] This was the opinion of Mr Ian McDonald, giving evidence to the Scott Enquiry in October 1993. 'The answer ... quite consciously side-stepped the precise point of the question ... but gave a truthful statement.'[6] This is hardly what most people would call truthful. Some would charitably call it 'dodging the issue' or 'telling little white lies'. Others would be more plain-spoken. At the same enquiry Sir Robin Butler, the Cabinet Secretary, said:

These are difficult lines to draw. It is not justified to mislead, but very often one finds oneself in a position where one has given an answer that is not the whole truth....[7]

This evasion of the whole truth is not confined to the occasional statement by senior civil servants – if it was, we would almost certainly understand and approve – but appears to be endemic and constantly practised, often with no apparent objective. Those who prepare the annual statement of defence estimates or draft statements for ministers to make to Parliament on such things as the Defence Costs Study must, of course, have half a mind at least on the effect that politicians wish to make and to tailor the emphasis accordingly. But often civil servants go beyond what is necessary. For example, some seem to play an elaborate game with the House of Commons Defence Committee, where the rules appear to be to say as little as possible in as many words as possible, whether or not it is necessary to obfuscate an issue.

I remember one particular session after the Falklands War when this game was being played. After what seemed several hours – we had not got very far – a Royal Marine colonel was asked a few questions by the Committee. He gave them clear, forceful, down-to-earth answers. The civil servants looked shocked, the Committee loved it, and it possibly saved several more sessions of beating about the bush. After a more recent visit, a senior civil servant said, 'Wasn't that fun? I think we probably won 1–0.'

Civil servants are of course masters of creative prose, of long minutes which say nothing. I well remember a civil servant, rather more down to earth than some, complaining about the written language of one of his subordinates: ' I am fairly well-read and I don't object to looking up in my dictionary a word or two from time to time, but I object to having to do so two or three times a page to understand what you really mean', was the substance of his rebuke. Of course busy people do not look up meanings of obscure words and a minute which may seem routine and bland can mean something very different. Potential opposition can often be circumvented by an apparently innocuous, highly devious statement, written or verbal. More often, though, it is done only for effect. Unfamiliar words become fashionable for a short while as everyone starts to use them to show they know what they mean or, more often, because they copy out of laziness.

Having worked in MOD for many years, I believed I knew reasonably well what we were about, but I was in for a shock. I believed we were carrying forward ministers' business, implementing the defence policy as outlined, however inadequately, by the Secretary of State for Defence and the Cabinet. I believed that civil servants worked alongside the military in this vital business, even if they carried their scrutiny and financial powers to absurd excess. But it seems I had been wrong all those years. At one high-powered meeting someone was putting forward a plan of action when a senior civil servant objected. It was explained that this was the only sensible course of action to implement policy. 'Ah!' he said, 'but our job is not to implement policy; our job is to protect ministers from embarrassment.'

I would have to agree that we cannot go about our business totally ignoring the risk of subsequent political embarrassment. This is obvious. But if we are only there to save ministers from embarrassment, most of us could go home and save the Treasury a great deal of money. The sad thing is that this was not a slip of the tongue or a badly worded statement but exactly what he and many others believe. Is it self-interest? Placing a minister in a difficult political situation is not very good for your future career; making a wrong decision over military equipment, when the responsibility can be shifted elsewhere very easily and when the real implications will not be clear to either public or politicians for a decade or more, is not such a black mark.

In the last chapter I mentioned the military promotion and selection systems which all too often place the wrong man in the job. Civil servants' selection and promotion, at least at the lower and middle grades, is in the hands of an outfit called Civilian Management, a large department in what was the Office of Management and Budget (OMB). Its record makes the military system look quite wonderful, though the latter often fails to get its act together. For all my criticism about selection policy, the Military Secretary's department has a very high strike rate in the nuts and bolts of selection and posting and it is rare that an officer gets less than a few months' notice. This is of course necessary when most military postings mean a move of house, often to another country, a move of school for the children and a change of job for the partner. All this takes time. Most civil servant job changes involve none of this as they will just move from one office in Whitehall to another, or at most from one London building to another. A great deal of advance notice is therefore not required. Nevertheless there are far too many instances where little or no notice is given. I first came across this when I was at the National Defence College at Latimer (sadly Latimer has since closed and the course moved to Greenwich, currently due for closure as well). Officers from the three Services formed the majority but there was a number of civil servants on the course. A few weeks before the end of this seven-month course, one of the civil servants was sent for by the Commandant and asked why he had not reported for duty in Whitehall that morning as his new branch was miffed at his non-arrival. He replied that he knew nothing about his new job, had not been contacted by anyone, had not been consulted over his preferences and had expected to receive his posting sometime during the remaining few weeks of the course. He left that day, but I rather doubt if he felt very motivated. With increasing rustication of traditionally London-based directorates, this inefficiency, if not corrected quickly, will cause increasing grief and unnecessary gaps. Many civil servants would agree that they are not well served by their management department. One military staff officer, incensed by Civilian Management's determination to place a bright, young, newly promoted executive officer into a totally unsuitable dead-end job, asked: 'What on earth is the word "management" doing in your title – you don't do any!' The bright, young, newly promoted executive officer resigned from the Civil Service two weeks later.

In contrast, the high-fliers are generally looked after pretty well – they are placed thoughtfully in posts of importance on the rungs of the longest and most vertical ladder on the board and well away from the snakes. Normally these posts do not require the incumbents to get their hands dirty, but when one finds himself in a real-life post, such as a financial post in the Procurement Executive where there is much scope for making spectacular cost estimation errors, he is frequently on his way – often on yet another promotion – before the implications come home to roost. There is a parallel here with the military: the 'golden boys' spend much time in private offices or secretariats of generals, permanent secretaries or ministers, and precious little time in lower-level posts where they have to hack through the complex detail of real life in the Procurement Executive, in Operational Requirements, in Army Staff Duties or in Civilian Management. They avoid this reality as far as possible and luxuriate like so many Bernards in arranging cars and Christmas card lists, and terrorising others with demands for massive briefs at a moment's notice to answer less than clearly enunciated requirements. Many majors and lieutenant colonels feel occasionally that they are at one with the majority of higher executive officers and principals.

Does all this matter? Does the mastery of the half-truth, and the minute which appears to say one thing and actually says another, make any real difference to decisions at the right point? In itself, this lack of principle probably does not, but it does lead the perpetrators to place great emphasis on their own power and we shall see in a later chapter how power, particularly over money, is an aim which is pursued to the extreme in an apparently laudable campaign to ensure that the taxpayers' money is not wasted. We shall see later how false that is.

Civil servants in MOD lack knowledge of the core business of the department, that is, defence. This probably applies in many other departments to a greater or lesser extent. How many of those in the Ministry of Agriculture, Food and Fisheries (MAFF) are experienced in trawling operations in the North Atlantic in rough weather? How many of those in the Home Office have been on the staff of a prison? How many of those in the Department of Health have worked in a hospital? Can those who have little detailed knowledge actually make sensible decisions on fishing, prisons and hospitals? I am not suggesting that the Department of Health should be populated exclusively with ex-nurses or MAFF with ex-trawlermen; but does it not make sense for at least some experts who know their field from the inside to be part of the department or ministry?

We have such experts in MOD: sailors, soldiers and airmen. Their views are based on in-depth knowledge of their Service, even if they are rather inflexible in their ideas and are not always very good at putting their case forward or at knowing their way around the Ministry and its arcane procedures. Civil servants have no such expertise. This does not matter so long as they stick to their side of the business and do not try to judge priorities in opposition to the military. But they do not, aided unconsciously by senior (and more junior) officers who all too often fail to state a clear priority or an unambiguous requirement. As Lord Bramall put it: 'The balance has swung disproportionately to the accountants.'

The fault does not only lie with the power-seeking civil servants but also with the less and less authoritative military. Too many of the middle-ranking officers in MOD today appear to accept that defeat by the civil servants is inevitable at every turn and give up the fight before it starts. This is not cowardice, just bewilderment at what they see as a lack of backbone by senior officers who often give away the prize without a fight after a hard scrap lower down the ladder. Why, therefore, start a fight in the first place if the generals are going to give way eventually? A peaceful capitulation first thing can save so much unnecessary effort.

This is causing a critical weakness in MOD. Not only are there still no post-Cold War concepts and very little new doctrine because of the difficulties of finding points of agreement rather than of disagreement between the Services and cap-badges; the lack of unanimity between them leads civil servants quite rightly to exploit the cracks in the arguments. In the absence of agreed concepts, decisions, particularly equipment decisions, are being reached more and more on a financial

basis rather than a requirement basis. Civil servants see nothing wrong with this as it is common practice in the civilian world: which major firm is not dominated by financiers and their financial arguments? But there is one major difference. In industry, the shareholders' money is at stake or, in the extreme, the future of the company and the employment of its work force, including the decision-makers, is threatened. In defence it is the lives of Servicemen that are at risk, not the lives of MOD decision-makers. I find it difficult to believe that civil servants ever remember this dimension – rows and columns of figures usually blot it out completely. But defence decisions are all about maximising deployable force within available funds, while minimising own casualties. Fundamental – but usually forgotten.

One example remains sharply etched in my mind. In July 1989, one civil servant refused to allow the spending of relatively small sums of money on some equipment which was essential for a new weapon system just about to enter Service. This equipment had been endorsed by the highest equipment committee and funding had been authorised by ministers as it was recognised that without it the new system was not battleworthy. The civil servant in question argued that this equipment was only an interim solution and that the final solution, which incidentally was also endorsed and funded, was only two years away. I explained patiently (too patiently perhaps) that we could not have in Service a major weapon system which was not operational. He said it was perfectly adequate for training purposes. My reply was that we purchase equipment to go to war. I got a little heated but he then took my breath away by saying: 'There will not be a war in the next two years and that is OMB policy.' It is a pity that no-one passed on the OMB's policy to Saddam Hussein who walked into Kuwait almost exactly a year after this ludicrous decision. The upshot was that we then had to make enormous efforts to persuade the United States to forego fitting some of their weapons with the interim solution so we could procure some and fit them before the ground war began. It was fortunate that we had much goodwill from the United States and a lot of time; if we had had less of either, one of our few battle-winning weapons could not have gone to war effectively.

In this case, the man was doing exactly what he thought was in the public interest, even though other scrutineers had endorsed the procurement and allocated funds and even though the highest MOD equipment committee had endorsed this position. He was not being obstructionist just for the sake of it. However, he had the power to reverse a high-level decision himself and because he had no direct war expertise and refused to consider the experts' view, he made an error. There are few with responsibility for procuring a particular piece of equipment yet many with no responsibility but with the power to say no. The case for having so many scrutineers, each with the power to veto, is often stated to be a proper safeguard of the public purse. However, as none of these veto-holding scrutineers has any war expertise, the question of soldiers' lives goes by default: the columns of figures are clearly more important.

In later chapters I shall make the case for wholesale reorganisation of MOD. Much of this affects the military, but the major impact falls on MOD headquarters civil servants who have escaped the axe time after time, despite the recent Defence Costs Study, despite logic. No doubt someone will suggest I look at how the Civil Service has been reduced over the last 15 years, particularly in MOD, and will produce figures to show how big the reductions have been. However, these figures hide a great deal. Much has been hived off as agencies or to the private sector (for example the Royal Ordnance factories and dockyards) and these reductions are counted proudly as progress. But the work is still being done – or, more importantly, the work that is left behind in MOD is still done by the same number of people. Nearly the same number, that is, because there have been some reductions. Most of these were in the industrial grades and in the scientific and technical Civil Service; the administrative mandarins and their staffs have remained comparatively untouched.

It will be interesting to see whether the 1994 White Paper on the future of the Civil Service will be, as *The Times* put it, 'the long delayed advent of a more credible conduct of business of government, or Sir Humphrey's last stand against creeping and inevitable reform'.[8]

The recently announced plan to open top jobs to competition to outsiders is pretty radical but generally welcomed. But will all jobs be opened up or just some? Will the core jobs remain closed? I am not in favour of a wholesale takeover by outsiders but some fresh air is surely needed in the rather over-cosy club. Without it there will be neither genuine reform nor genuine reduction in numbers where it is needed most.

If the real aim of MOD's civil servants is not to implement ministers' policies but to save them embarrassment, the consequent translation is that mistakes must not be made. This in turn leads to the objective of not making any decisions, or rather stopping any decisions being made. If this is impossible, then better to avoid accountability. And this is perhaps the crux of the matter.

A leader in *The Times* at the time of the Scott Enquiry stated that Sir Robin Butler's 'remarks this week have epitomised the distaste many civil servants still feel for public scrutiny in general'. I would take this further: civil servants feel distaste for clear accountability. They are happy to order military men and scientists to sign their name to procurement details, but they are not at all keen on signing their names to their own decisions. Graham Mather, President of the European Policy Forum, was quoted in *The Times* as saying:

> *Lawyers and doctors face the constant threat of negligence claims, which has the effect of concentrating the mind. But there is no equivalent discipline in Whitehall. Senior civil servants do not lose sleep out of fear that they might be held responsible for their actions.*[9]

Indeed Nicholas Soames, in the interview already quoted, lent his weight to the defence of the Civil Service: 'There's no point turning round and blaming officials when it all goes wrong, because civil servants just give advice.' Maybe they do. But they should be implementing ministers' policy and, if they get that wrong, they ought to be held accountable. As we shall see later, it is the lack of accountability that so bedevils life in MOD.

A Walk on the Rough Side (1991)

This walk in South London was taken in 1991 and the description is of the area and the streets as they appeared at that time. Since then, relatively little has changed. Perhaps the most obvious change has been to the OXO tower block which is now finished. Other changes have been made but are less obvious.

ॐ

Down the steps at Waterloo, through the stench of urine, past the patient strag-gling bus queues on the right, out into the relative freshness of the Waterloo Road and on into the back streets of Southwark. Past the Union Jack Club and under the railway line near Waterloo East where devoted mechanics work on vin-tage Citroën cars in minuscule workshops under the brick arches. Into Roupell Street with a flowing tide of humanity moving east from Waterloo to their work at either end of Blackfriars Bridge, a clatter of stiletto heels, the heavier clump of tra-ditional black shoes, briefcases of all styles and not a rolled umbrella in sight.

Roupell Street is a cosy thoroughfare of terraced houses, its apparently sleepy character disturbed only during the morning and evening rush hours by the human river which slides past the doors and by the loudspeaker on Waterloo East, just above the small gardens of the houses on the south side, booming information about the next train to arrive at Platform C or depart from Platform A. At other times it basks in the summer sun or huddles tightly in the winter rain. A residential street typical of South London, poor, mean, dilapidated, human – or it was until recently. Too near to the fringes of the City to remain in an 1850s time warp, it is now being 'improved' piecemeal, as smart executives buy, renovate and move into lower-cost, convenient pieds-à-terre: executive cars outside, executive decoration inside, exec-utive movement and dress between door and car contrast starkly with the peeling paint of doors that open to allow a little old lady who has probably lived there all her life to put out the milk bottles with her cat, or to reveal an elderly pensioner about to shuffle down to the corner shop in his slippers for his paper and tobacco.

There used to be a corner shop at the Waterloo end of Roupell Street but it is now a classy delicatessen, symptomatic of the street's changing lifestyle. Halfway up and opposite The King's Arms pub are two more shops. Some time ago, one became a Persian carpet vendor; I gave it a year to survive and was about right. How a lux-ury shop expected to make sales in an area where no-one would look for a carpet I don't know but I suppose it hoped to catch the eye of the commuters. A vain hope as commuters' eyes are usually closed – at least metaphorically. Now it is an art gallery which never appears to be open. The other shop was a ski outfitters, but it seems to have gone down the slippery slope and is empty. The only shop which appears to thrive is at the far end: a newsagent/confectioner corner shop which the commuters and residents patronise alike.

At the top end of Roupell Street in an easterly direction is Meymott Street. where huge new buildings are rising. Until recently this little area was a wilderness with The Rose and Crown sticking up amongst Second World War desolation like one sound tooth in an otherwise empty gum; a haven of wild life – butterflies, beetles, buddleia and nettles abounded. All this life is now doomed as construction is about to begin. Opposite this open space stands a telephone exchange which for years bore the strange graffiti: '99% IS SHIT'. But 99 per cent of what? Hardly an objection to a pay rise, or a description of the Thames! Could it be a statement on the quality of BT management or a commentary on the human race by some poor, downtrodden individual? Or perhaps it is aimed at the executives moving into the area? It remains clearly visible despite attempts to obliterate it.

The new block at the end of the street replaces a dilapidated row of houses which were for long under sentence of death. During the lingering death throes several temporary shops came and went, including a local press and a hairdresser named 'Air Aid, appropriately, in view of the proximity to reminders of 1940s air raids. None of them flourished any more or less than the branch office of some obscure trade union at the end of the street with its fly-blown windows, its unwashed, half-filled tea mugs and its 1930s-style posters.

But I am in a hurry for there is much work of national importance to do and my path lay not along Meymott Street but along Hatfields, past the small allotment patch with its thriving roses and vegetables, alongside the scruffy little park with its litter of bonfire ashes and old women watching their dogs' daily doings, on by the seemingly deserted warehouses and the din of the school playground and across the Stamford Street traffic jam, shoulder to shoulder now with smartly dressed ladies, heading for the giant building housing IPC magazines – the 'largest consumer magazine publishing house in Europe' – most of them looking like secretaries or receptionists, but some of the maturer variety hinting at agony aunts or knitting experts.

By this building and parallel to the river runs Upper Ground, formerly a Service road for the old warehouses along the south bank of the Thames between Waterloo and Blackfriars Bridge. Most of these have gone and have been replaced by a park, a small market, flats and the huge bulk of Sea Containers House which stretches from the historic inn – The Coat and Badge – to the last remaining bastion of decrepitude: the crumbling block around the Shot Tower with its blatant OXO advert built into the windows. 'That's not advertising, it's a modern abstract design', they said at the time. But Bernard Levin and others campaigned for its survival and the block remains shored up, walled up, eyeless and an eyesore.

Not until Blackfriars Bridge is underfoot are we out of the huddle of South London. Suddenly there are spacious views to east and west, from the Houses of Parliament to St Paul's Cathedral, from Somerset House and the Temple to London Bridge and the high-rise City buildings. Another tide of humanity crosses the river, on the western side in a northerly direction from the stations and bus stops of Southwark to work in Blackfriars and Fleet Street, and on the eastern side in a southerly direction from Blackfriars to the glossy new *Daily Express* building rising from the sliver of waste British Rail ground alongside the railway bridge, cursed no doubt for obliterating the view by the managers on the top floors of the 1970s Lloyds Bank building next door.

The clicking of high heels and the clumping of men's shoes merges into the bustling hum of traffic. There is little communication, however, as each commuter is silently locked into his or her own little world of somnolence, vacuity or anxiety, unable to recognise anyone or anything, intent on the next few yards of pavement and the backs of those immediately in front. Even the crowded buses are aurally a desert. What thoughts there may be are concentrated on the excitement of last night or the coming boredom of the day.

It is surprising to hear at my shoulder: 'Hi, Maureen! Late again? The old dragon won't be pleased!' Maureen turns her head, eyes brighter, a smile appears. 'Hi, Sharon! Didn't hear my alarm again.' Black and white go off arm in arm, no longer two automatons trudging wearily to work, but friends in a slowly brightening world. Another apparently normal day.

Down into the Blackfriars Underpass, more urinal smells. A solid stream of humans and it is difficult to know whether it is easier going with or against it. Up the steps by the Unilever Building onto New Bridge Street. Into all this normal bustling a strange note obtrudes. An *Evening Standard* van pulls up and at 8 a.m. the first editions of the evening paper are dumped at the newspaper kiosk. There is little to show that anyone has noticed. There should be, and perhaps is, interest under the surface, but more likely the lack of reaction is just ignorance which will quickly be dispelled by massive media coverage in the weeks to come. I quicken my steps still further. It is 16 January 1991 and Britain is at war in the Gulf.

CHAPTER FOUR

The Scientists and Science

The scientist everywhere has acquired an aura of sanctity – or satanity – in the last half-century. In the defence field he has acquired something of a major divinity.

DAVID DIVINE, THE BLUNTED SWORD, 1964[1]

The military, by and large, has always been suspicious of scientists, even of military officers with scientific degrees. In the 1920s General Haig was extolling the virtues of the horse on the battlefield as opposed to the new-fangled tank and aeroplane, and the Army was reluctant to embrace anything which would displace it. Liddell-Hart was very much a voice in the wilderness. The Second World War changed all that and the scientific advances made during that half-decade, culminating in the dropping of the atom bombs on Japan, made scientists central to the whole defence effort. Although suspicion of them continued, and it is alive and well in today's Army, scientists were accepted as a necessary evil, acceptable so long as they were miles away in Whitehall, or Malvern, or Farnborough. They were not welcome on operations where they would 'be in the way'. These attitudes surfaced in the Falklands War and again in the Gulf War with the result that precious data on weapon and force performance were not collected.

This prejudice will not be overcome until scientists are attached permanently, in peace as well as war, to every large headquarters, and until every commander knows 'his' scientists and is able to trust them. This should be no surprise as it is in fact only an extension of the regimental system, the Army's most sacred cow. If you are to rely on your colleagues in the heat of battle, you must be able to trust them; if you are to trust them, you must know them and understand their strengths and weaknesses. So it is with scientists. The appearance of a strange person, labelled 'scientist', just before battle is joined is hardly the way to a fruitful relationship.

In 1964, David Divine saw the defence scientist as part way to a major divinity. Since then, they have gone further and their power and influence now extend right across the procurement field: the Chief Scientific Adviser chairs the top equipment procurement committee; his staff scrutinise and can veto all committee submissions; operational analysis has taken the place of military judgement; and the Procurement Executive is set on a path towards complete civilianisation, which means procurement by scientists and engineers. Military influence is being throttled, with the willing, albeit unconscious, co-operation of the Army at large. The

only recent setback to scientific dominance came in 1992 with the creation of the Defence Research Agency and the change to military direction of the applied research programme. Although it was opposed bitterly by many scientists, military direction, in close co-operation with the scientists, has worked well. But with the opening provided by the Defence Costs Study, the scientists have struck back and are busy reimposing their own control on the applied research programme.

Nothing epitomises the shift in balance more than the role of operational analysis. Military judgement is no longer accepted in committee papers – 'he would say that, wouldn't he?' – and it is perhaps significant that the senior equipment committee is composed of three civilians and one military officer. The latter is a rotational post, which means that the final decision on a new tank, for example, may well be taken by a committee without the expertise that would be provided by an Army officer. The same may be true for a new aircraft or a new frigate. Military judgement is not considered important; operational analysis is.

But those who understand operational analysis and are honest about it will be the first to agree that it cannot provide the definitive answers senior MOD men expect from it. Neither can it provide useful answers on a short time scale. The larger the question, the longer it takes and the more nebulous is the answer. Ask: 'Will this anti-tank missile be more effective than that one in these scenarios?' and you will be given clear, believable answers in less than a year. Ask: 'Is it better to invest in another frigate rather than in an Army operational command and control system?' and the analysts can, after a long, costly study, only give you very general guidance, with many caveats.

In 1964 E.S. Quade wrote:

There is a tendency to associate analysis with credibility – particularly if the magic word 'computer' is mentioned. The real threat lies not so much in deliberate deceit as it does in subconscious desires to substantiate one's previously committed position.[2]

Those were relatively early days, but has much changed? Many people in MOD today would certainly agree with the above statement. So would some experts in the field. In 1991, Davis and Blumenthal stated:

The vast majority of the model community are relatively too enthusiastic about the advances in computer performance, communications and human interfaces, and much too little interested in the substance *of the models and the validity of the lessons that will be learned from them. The models are in many cases built on a base of sand.*[3]

Despite this, senior scientists have cynically pedalled operational analysis as the magic formula for decision-making. While this has been opposed by the military, who see it correctly as just one aid in the decision-making process, it has been embraced enthusiastically by the administrative civil servants as an easy way out of difficult decisions. If the analysis fits with the financial view, they can endorse it and shovel accountability onto the scientists. If it does not fit, they can always ask for another study, and another until the 'right' answer appears. Some senior scientists are, sadly, more politically-minded than they should be, yet they are generally not very good at Whitehall politics. Should this be a surprise to us?

The scientific civil service attracts high-quality scientists who want to do research work. Many are very good at it, as is evident from the wide range of work in some MOD research establishments that has led the world in so many fields. They have an extraordinary pride in their work, they work absurdly long hours at critical points in the research programme, they are real experts in their field, and they are professionals. Regrettably much of this is at risk as the Defence Research Agency introduces 'progressive' management methods that inundate everybody with paper and treat the individual as a machine. Will the scientists' professional pride survive this faceless assault?

Being professionals with an intense interest in their own fields, scientists are often guilty of partiality in their own advice: their product is better than anyone else's; other scientific experts are mistaken, their views erroneous; the 'not-invented-here' is rooted firmly in the subconscious. I remember heading the British delegation to a highly technical meeting in the United States. For a week my scientific experts appeared happy with the US presentations. On return to the United Kingdom, I expressed satisfaction that the US view was so coincident with ours. 'Not at all', came the reply, 'the US so-called experts clearly knew nothing, so it wasn't worthwhile discussing anything!' Not-invented-here was alive and well.

The whole scientific world breaks down when scientists are promoted from research to management posts. With few exceptions, scientists are hopeless managers. This should be no surprise as the qualities required for successful management are very different from those required for successful world-class research. Away from the scientific coal-face, scientists are often like fish out of water.

Despite this, more and more scientists are being taken from the bench and stuffed into posts managing costs, resources, plans, policy and the general bureaucratic day-to-day trivia. We need scientists where they contribute best – in the forefront of research. Others who are better suited should do the management. This would be unpopular with the scientists, though. Their budgets have been cut again and again, and they feel that they need to maximise scientific posts – any job will serve. The proportion of scientific researchers to scientific managers is decreasing all the time as 'resource management' takes the place of scientific supervision.

This is one reason for the decline in the number of scientists. The other reason is even more dominant: the low level of MOD research spending. While research funding appears to have held up well over the last few turbulent years, it is low in comparison with other major Western nations. Figures which compare accurately like with like are difficult to obtain, but government figures show that in France 3.3 per cent of the defence budget is spent on research as compared to 2.2 per cent in the United States and 1.9 per cent in the United Kingdom. While the comparison with the United States is not unflattering superficially, the actual money available for research on this side of the Atlantic is an order of magnitude or two lower. The comparison with France is more telling.

Compare what we spend on research with some other areas:[4]

Defence budget (p.a.)	£23,000m
MOD research	£500m
OMB running costs	£1,200m
CDP running costs	£1,000m
(excluding equipment procurement)	
Whitehall office computers (1990–4)	£4,000m
Whitehall office computers (1995–2000)	£6,000m
Eurofighter procurement	£13,000m

This seems to me to show two things. Firstly, the overall spending on research is very small: about one-quarter of what is spent on the running costs of just two of the major areas in MOD and about half of what is spent on office computers in Whitehall every year. Secondly, we could increase the research budget significantly without much effect elsewhere; if we doubled it, the defence budget would grow by only two per cent. Such an increase would surely be lost in the noise.

Comparison with other nations is also interesting. The United States spend nearly ten times the amount we do on research, France almost twice as much. How can we keep up with these other leaders in the defence field if we do not increase our research budget, or worse, if we continue to reduce it further as we seem to be set to do?

Does British industry fill the gap? Figures here are even more elusive than with government spending and I can find no firm basis from which to argue. However, the general feeling is that the British defence industry spends between half and two per cent of its annual turnover on private venture research. A general claim, unsubstantiated as far as I can tell, is that this is significantly below similar budgets in other major Western nations.

A comparison between the British defence industry and the British civil industry is also interesting. British defence firms, on average, contribute themselves only about a quarter of the funds for their research and development, most of it coming from the government defence budget, whereas in the civil sector companies contribute around 80 per cent of the funding for their research and development programme.[5] A good example of the divide is the Glaxo Wellcome new research centre at Stevenage which cost £700m – presumably this did not come out of Glaxo's £1.2bn annual research and development budget.[6]

The defence industry will no doubt claim that government defence equipment policy is making it impossible to invest in research on any useful scale; and that the cost of competition, the reduction in government-funded development and the frequency with which foreign firms are awarded plum contracts are bankrupting them slowly. But did they do any better in the early 1980s when, at the height of cost-plus contracting, the defence industry was generally believed to be 'ripping off' MOD? The figures I have suggest not. Another claim the defence industry might make is that they are hamstrung by the short-termism of the City and the shareholders. This is indeed a serious constraint, but does the civil sector not also have this constraint?

I believe that the defence industry grew fat and idle on government money until the mid-1980s when the game was up. There is little tradition of self-funded research and it is a bad time to start major expenditure with long-term payoffs when facing up to the gnashing of short-term shareholders' teeth. Yet if the defence industry does not invest in the future, it will not survive. You can only live in the marketplace either by producing better and more cheaply what everyone produces, or by producing what somebody wants but nobody else provides. The improvement in efficiency of the British defence industry over the last ten years presents a gleam of hope, but the only safe way to future salvation is through quality research and development. British scientists are traditionally unequalled in this sphere but they need the money to be able to deliver the goods. This money will not come in increasing quantities from the government but will have to be found from industry's own pocket. Whether this is now possible I do not know. I would, however, look very closely at certain areas which may or may not contribute a great deal to overall effectiveness, the two main areas being managerial overheads and the marketing budget.

Whether or not industry manages to increase its research budget, MOD needs the maximum research for the limited funding available, and that research must be directed clearly towards a useful end result. In general the direction is good and will continue to be so given military direction – for it is only the military which can decide the shape of the future equipment programme towards which all research must be aimed. Any move by the scientific community to claim that direction back must be resolutely resisted. It is not that the scientists are unimportant. They are in fact crucial to the success of the research programme, but they must do what they do best, which is research, not management. There should be a very close and harmonious relationship, with the military deciding priorities and general direction and the scientists producing and carrying out a programme to suit. Currently it works better than it has done for some decades.

Military direction and scientific excellence will give us good value. What is likely to undermine that value is something that can most usefully be called management overheads. The Defence Research Agency was set up to trade, on a quasi-commercial basis, with its major customer, MOD. Contracts, deliverables, payment milestones, outturn forecasts, bill payments and a host of other such activities now crowd out science from the agendas of committees and meetings. Forms A, B, C, D, E, RM 1, RM 2 and probably as many or more again clutter up the working life of the scientific managers within the Defence Research Agency and within MOD. There is no time to supervise research. Mindnumbing bureaucracy rules supreme. Whether this bureaucracy has the right effect and whether it aids accountability will be looked at in a later chapter. It is sufficient to say here that there is a real and increasing danger of the vital scientific decisions within the Defence Research Agency being taken by inexperienced researchers at too low a level and constrained only by financial and other 'management' factors.

This danger has been recognised and 'technical consultants' have been created in some areas within the Defence Research Agency in an attempt to overcome the problem, leaving the resource managers – who are experienced scientists – waist-deep in paper. There are also customer 'points-of-contact'. So who is really in charge? Is it the points of contact, or the person who oversees the research, or the person who manages the resources? I wish I knew. An equally pertinent point is the ratio of scientific workers, both researchers and supervisors, to resource and other managers. What is it and can it be justified? All this is a tragedy, for it crucially undermines the very real advances made by the scientists since the formation of the Defence Research Agency. It is crucial because without any doubt we spend far too little on defence research. To spend too high a proportion of too little on 'management' compounds the problem. We have large numbers of excellent scientists – why waste their talents in jobs for which they are unsuited?

We spend too little on research, and we could spend significantly more without upsetting the defence budget more than marginally. Unless we do, our country and our defence industry will be in very serious trouble in ten to fifteen years time. We already have a fraction of the tank or artillery strengths of large numbers of third world countries. Will we be forced in the future, like they are now, to rely on other nations to supply us with our equipment?

CHAPTER FIVE

Procedures and Working Practices

I should deprecate setting up a special committee. We are overrun with them,
like the Australians were by the rabbits.

WINSTON CHURCHILL[1]

The Ministry of Defence is large. In addition to the military, civil servants and scientists populate numerous buildings in London, Bristol and many places elsewhere. In the Main Building in Whitehall alone, there are three miles of corridors joining around 1,000 offices populated by some 3,800 workers. The civilian contingent is larger than the size of the post-Options Army or roughly four times the size of the ground and air forces we deployed in the Gulf War, a force which we are now unlikely to be able to sustain in any future operation of this kind. To put it in financial terms, the annual spend on all Army equipment (from tanks, helicopters and self-propelled howitzers to trunk and radio communications equipment, from bridging and mines to airborne and ground-based surveillance sensors, from infantry weapons and air defence missiles to target acquisition radars and night sights, from command and control information systems and special forces equipment to logistic vehicles and chemical defence equipment and much else besides) is roughly the same as the annual running costs of what used to be called the Office of Management and Budget (OMB) in MOD.[2] Or put another way, we spend more on just some of those civil servants who manage and account for defence expenditure than we do on equipping the Army.

Can this really be the case? The answer is yes, as it is shown clearly in the *Statement on the Defence Estimates* for 1996. These figures also show that the budget for administration was set to decline, but it is difficult to see by how much because of reorganisation since the Defence Costs Study. What is certain is that there are more accounting civil servants elsewhere – in Service headquarters, in garrisons, in research establishments, in the Central Staffs and in the Procurement Executive. The cost, incidentally, of running the Procurement Executive before any equipment is procured is only just less than the total spend on the Army equipment listed above. Moreover, the budget for office computers in Whitehall is of the same order. We spend about as much on running MOD as we spend on equipping the Army and the Royal Navy together.

In my opinion, this illustrates incontrovertibly the size and the cost of the MOD. The question is: can we really afford such a monster if all we get is the ability to sustain less than a division in a major operation while supporting simultaneously the current force levels in Northern Ireland? There is no simple answer to this, although the temptation is to say that such levels of manpower and expenditure on central management are obviously unjustifiable. But be careful! There must be sizeable overheads whatever the scale of the armed force that is deployable, and as the overall defence budget is reduced, these overheads must become a larger proportion of the total budget. A small reduction in the overall budget could mean a far larger proportional cut in the resources available for manning and equipping the Services in the field. This was certainly the case in Options for Change and it was so clear that the Defence Costs Study was an obvious necessity to tip the scales a little in the opposite direction.

The question is not whether we can afford the necessary defence overheads, but whether those overheads are as low as possible without either endangering operations or taking undue risks with the taxpayers' money. In February 1993, David Hart argued that the British fighting Services were not giving value for money – there was not enough 'bang for our bucks'. He claimed:

We have a quite extraordinary number of senior officers compared with other nations. The ratio of British general officers to total servicemen is 1:420. In the United States and in France it is 1:1900. In Germany it is 1:2300. The British Navy has as many admirals as ships. The RAF has an excessively top heavy command structure.[3]

He produced the following table to back his argument.

Table 1
Comparative Fighting Capacity

Country	Budget ($bn)	Combat Aircraft	Fleet Units	Main Battle Tanks	Armed Helicopters	Armoured Fighting Vehicles	Artillery Pieces (tubed)
UK	41.2	511	161	1,312	291	6,083	762
France	34.9	910	148	1,343	720	6,268	1,436
Israel	6.76	662	64	3,890	93	8,480	1,420

Note: All figures from *Military Balance* 1992/93.

These figures represent the state in 1992. Since then, we have been pressing ahead with the massive reductions under Options for Change, so that we now have less than one-third of the tanks shown above. The balance, or rather imbalance, is even more unflattering. Much but not all of the top-heavy structure which reduces the 'bang for our bucks' is in MOD.

MOD is divided into the 'doers' and the 'accountants', as Lord Bramall put it. It is difficult to arrive at any clear indication of the ratio between the two groups. Some would be tempted to define the 'doers' as the military and the 'accountants' as the civil servants. This is clearly wrong as many civil servants are 'doers' and many military, if not 'accountants', do not contribute much, if anything. For example, some of the civil servants in several of the branches of the OMB are very definitely 'doers' as any sensible system would grind to a halt without them. Most of the scientists in the procurement branches of the Procurement Executive are 'doers'. Conversely, some military posts, notably in specialist areas such as Command and Information Systems and Human Factors, add little or nothing to progress. My own extremely limited research indicates that at the very maximum no more than 48 per cent of MOD are 'doers' or involved in making progress, while more than half are concerned with supporting the structure or scrutinising, that is, in the words of the civil servant quoted earlier, ensuring that ministers are not embarrassed. A rather more hard-nosed study would put the 'doers' at less than 20 per cent of the total MOD.

There are two major issues. The first is manning levels, which vary enormously. Many of the most important branches in MOD are high profile and, because they are obvious targets and their role understood, have been cut at each turn of the budgetary screw. Some are now below viable levels and only keep going through the dedication of their staff. I would cite examples of some Resources & Programmes (RP) branches in OMB, Operational Requirements and some project teams in the Procurement Executive. In Operational Requirements (Land), desk officers work extremely long hours at high pressure even when they have no major committee submission on their hands; when they start working on submissions, the very heart of their work, officers have little time for the remainder of their responsibilities for six to twelve months. The result is that work towards future equipment submissions is delayed or skimped. In other words, these officers are already totally saturated without their major core business.

But elsewhere the situation is the opposite. One Army branch had about 15 people working in one area of non-operational equipment – compare this with one desk officer dealing with all the equivalent operational Army equipment, a roughly equal responsibility. One Army officer in a particularly vague area under a senior scientist recorded the average time he spent doing his job in 1994 as 41 minutes per day; for the rest of the time, he had nothing to do. A wing commander elsewhere told me he always finished his day's work by 10 a.m. in the morning. And is there really any need for 177 executive grades and goodness knows how many clerical staff just paying bills when the scrutiny of, and accounting for, expenditure is the responsibility of three or four financial armies elsewhere? It is hard to see what these highly paid executives do except to duplicate or triplicate responsibilities. It is less hard to see why these people remain: no-one is likely to try very hard to disestablish their 'cushy' numbers or to cut work that is only duplicating what is done elsewhere; if they did, their bosses would oppose it. Administrative man is by nature an empire builder, numbers of subordinates equating to perceived power.

Above the 'doers' sits a plethora of branches variously labelled 'plans', 'policy', 'secretariat' and so on. Most of these are staffed liberally. Few produce anything useful. Most initiate a stream of 'initiatives', 'procedures', 'guidelines' and 'ratio-nalisation' ideas. Many shield the 'great men' from reality. Paper flows, work amongst the 'doers' goes off the top of the graph, but few useful results can be ascertained. Part although not all of the problem is that these branches, which often sit close to senior officers and civil servants, are overstaffed with energetic, ambitious people too often lacking the adequate intellect for the job. It might be this combination of ambition and lack of intellectual capacity, combined with plenty of peer competition in the same corridor, which is the lethal combination. In summary, although there is some critical undermanning, there is much more overmanning, a lot of it serious. It is perhaps not as bad as NATO headquarters in Brussels, but bad nevertheless.

The second major reason for MOD size is the way it goes about its business. Defence is a most complex business costing over £20bn of the taxpayers' money each year and this money has to be spent wisely. There cannot be waste, there cannot be big mistakes. Safeguards, scrutiny and checks are all important, but they inevitably add to the running costs and the manpower bill. They are necessary, but can they be retained at less cost in resources? Can the system be improved?

The letter of implementation of the Defence Costs Study No 1 made the point that the reduction of MOD head office would be critically dependent on the adoption of new working and management practices that would reduce the more time-consuming routine staff work and enable the smaller staffs to discharge their responsibilities more effectively. It went on to announce that a review would be carried out early in 1995 into the MOD formal committee structure to tackle the common complaint at all levels that the committee culture was leading to a lack of decisions and poor compromise solutions.

All this is wholeheartedly welcome – if delivered; there are as yet no signs of a forthcoming birth. But this official statement highlights not only the routine staff work to which I will return later, but the widely held view that there are too many committees where consensus is required to reach decisions and where consensus can be reached only by compromise. Everyone is agreed that this must change. Churchill would have agreed, too.

Why are there so many committees and so many consensus-driven compromise decisions? Apart from the fact that many people feel 'comfortable' with them because they can shuffle off responsibility, apart from the fact that many people have grown up in a culture which forms a committee to tackle every new problem, the real reason is that, sadly, it is necessary. It is necessary because few, if any, major decisions are the responsibility of one person. It is the whole business of 'accountability' that is at the bottom of the problem. As has been said earlier, there are those who have responsibility without power and those who have power without responsibility; the former tend to be the 'doers', the latter the 'accountants' but also – more and more in the equipment world – scientific scrutineers. But it is not a battle between one 'doer' with responsibility and one 'accountant' with power. It is nearly always a battle between several 'doers' and many 'accountants', each with his own perspective. Decisions can only be sorted out round a table; hence the committee.

Let us look at accountability more closely. Let us assume that a serious capability gap has appeared, or is about to appear, in the Army equipment programme: an armoured vehicle of some type is coming to the end of its useful life. Its running costs are about to go through the roof, its armour is too light to protect the crew, its mobility too poor to keep up with the new tanks, its firepower inadequate against new enemy armour and its night surveillance and weapon sights too old to be used at the ranges currently necessary. The replacement, which was originally planned to be delivered from the factory production line about now, has suffered a series of delays and is still ten years away from deployment. For ten years, therefore, the Army will be forced to use, and pay for, the inadequate in-service vehicle and may well lose lives in any conflict during this time, lives which would not have been lost if the new vehicle had been completed on time. Who is to blame for this 'unnecessary' loss of life?

A very good question! Is it the professional head of the Army, the Chief of the General Staff, who is ultimately responsible for delivering the Army capability? No, for while he is nominally in charge of what equipment the Army spends its money on, many of the delays and reductions which are imposed along the way are done so without his, or his staff's, involvement. Is it the Deputy Chief of the Defence Staff (Programmes and Planning), who has the final military say each year on what stays in the programme, what goes and what is delayed, and who may have insisted on this particular project being delayed at various times over the last decade to keep the overall programme within available resources? Or is it his civilian opposite number, the Deputy Under Secretary (Programmes)? No, for neither has control over what goes into the equipment programme in the first place and, while their influence is massive, by themselves they can only shape the programme marginally each year. Is it the Chief of Defence Procurement, who is responsible for the development of the equipment and the technical delays that may have taken place during development? No, for he is not responsible for centrally imposed programme delays. Is it the Operational Requirements staff who took such a long time to produce a staff target in the first place? No, for they had no control over the concepts or doctrine staff who failed year after year to come up with the necessary starting point for detailed equipment policy to be produced. Was it the central scientific staff who produced ambiguous high-level operational analysis studies which gave no clear indication that replacement was a high priority in the time scale? No, because they had used, in the absence of anything official, concepts and doctrine which were later discredited. Was it ... ? You could go on and on. The answer is that no single person was responsible: numbers of people have made isolated decisions which in themselves are entirely defensible but which, when strung together, cause a serious capability gap to open up and lives to be placed at risk. Not only is no single person responsible, but no specific group or committee can be held accountable. Even if all the factors over the ten years are listed, it is unlikely that any one of those could be clearly identified as the main cause of the problem.

The maze of decision-making is well illustrated by the diagram opposite of the procurement process. I do not intend to describe the detail or even unravel the mysteries of abbreviations, as I believe the overall picture makes the point. At first sight it looks as if it is meant as a joke, but it is a good representation of the process. It appears to be the only effort anyone has made to demonstrate the intricacies and farcicalities of the present system. It shows quite clearly that no-one is accountable.

If no-one is accountable, no-one can be sacked. Anyone can therefore take a decision knowing that they are extremely unlikely to be penalised in any way if it is wrong. If they lack the knowledge to assess the real implications themselves and if they forget, as many civil servants seem to, that eventually soldiers' lives are at risk, it is hardly surprising if important decisions are taken more lightly than they should be.

Most equipment decisions are taken in two parts. While the Equipment Approvals Committee will endorse (or not) expenditure on a given system against a particular requirement with a particular procurement strategy, this decision cannot be made until adequate funds for the whole life of the system are provided in the long-term costings (LTC). It is during the annual LTC cycle that all important decisions about the funding of equipment and delay to that funding are taken. While the LTC process begins as a stately dance with measured decisions, the pace hots up throughout the autumn until, in late November and December, far-reaching decisions are made on a moment's thought and with minimal facts available. A desk officer, faced with a lightning decision by the powers-that-be to cancel this or delay that, may well think: 'It took ten years to build my programme, but just ten minutes to cut it to ribbons.'

Over the 12 months or more of each annual cycle, vast numbers of people and committees are involved. This annual exercise can have a disastrous effect on programmes yet it is a financial exercise, governed primarily by where that project's funding lies in the ten-year programme: the project can be delayed year after year by the central programme staff on purely financial grounds often late in the process

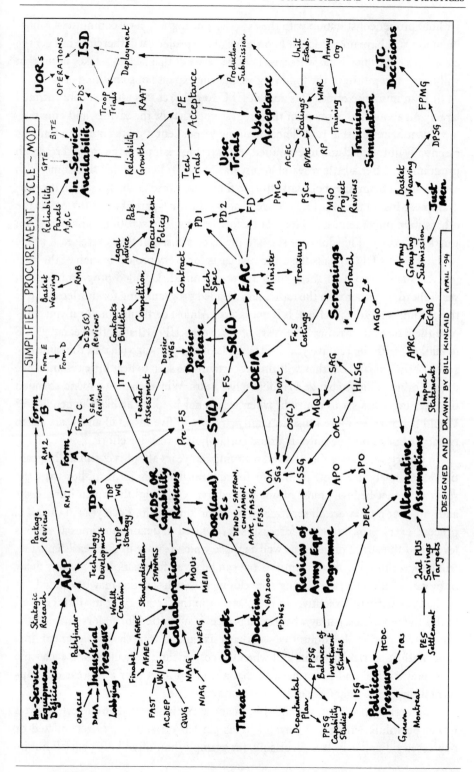

SIMPLIFIED PROCUREMENT CYCLE ~ MOD

DESIGNED AND DRAWN BY BILL KINCAID   APRIL '94

without proper consultation with the experts. The highest-level committees, whose members will have no particular knowledge of the project, will therefore not get the clear advice they need and worse, will not be aware of that lack. Mistakes occur that will have to be put right the following year at the expense of something else.

It is an immense effort, this annual LTC round. Yet this effort is concentrated largely on about five per cent of the programme, that is, the savings and enhancement candidates for that year. The remaining 95 per cent is costed but then remains essentially untouched and unexamined. An extreme example is the applied research programme. After a little research of my own in 1994, I concluded that some £3m each year was being spent on staff effort to find and prioritise savings within the programme. Most of the effort was concentrated on a small part of those savings as the others were uncontentious. This £3m effort was made to scrutinise less than £3m worth of savings. This does not seem to me to be a cost-effective exercise.

Each year's LTC details the estimated costs for every project in each of the next ten years and every year these costs are re-examined. Detailed programming ten years ahead, together with the rather less detailed programming for the decade after that, requires huge staff effort. Is it necessary? Almost certainly not, for if you compare the figures for the first five years of this year's LTC (that is, the years 1997/8 to 2001/2) with the last five years of the LTC of five years ago (that is, the same five years 1997/8 to 2001/2) they will almost certainly be seen to bear little resemblance to each other. Things change so much in five years. Why then do we spend so much time getting years six to ten right when we cannot predict the likely expenditure? Would it not make more sense to plan years one to five in detail and years six to twenty in rough outline only? It would certainly save massive effort.

In theory, of course, the detailed planning ten years ahead is essential. In practice it cannot be done other than in form. And it is this form, rather than the substance, that bedevils most of our procedures. Quite rightly expenditure, costs and value for money are all scrutinised time and time again. Each year in the LTC process, every project budget forecast is scrutinised in detail four times at various levels and the larger projects, as well as those which feature in that year's cuts list, will be scrutinised again to identify what can be saved for example by a year's delay or by cancellation halfway through development. Such scrutiny may be carried out in the Procurement Executive, in the OMB or in the Treasury, or in all three. Add to this the repeated scrutiny whenever a project is submitted for endorsement to the Equipment Approvals Committee – perhaps six times during the development time scale, both at particular points and when the cost or time scale increases, each time at several levels – and it can be seen that a major project over a 15-year developmental time scale might be scrutinised some 150 times.

You might expect that, after all this, financial costings would be correct, but you would be wildly wrong. All sorts of items get left off and others get inflated or depressed ridiculously. It is surprising, for example, how often VAT gets left out by

mistake; how often spares levels are assessed incorrectly; how often training equipment is ignored. But repeated financial scrutiny fails to identify these errors year after year for the simple reason that it is all done very superficially. There is no in-depth financial audit at any point. The costings are produced by mere number-crunchers, individuals with little or no knowledge of the particular equipment or indeed of any equipment. Their costings need checking. They do not get it. Instead we have what I call 'tick-in-the-box' scrutiny.

A good example of the 'tick-in-the-box' mentality concerns the Treasury scrutiny of a project some years ago. The Equipment Approvals Committee, or rather its forerunner, had endorsed both the project requirement document and the funds for development after intense scrutiny by all interested parts of MOD, and it was now the turn of the Treasury to crawl all over the papers.

I was rung up by an official from the Treasury who said that the operational case was not convincing. This was a little surprising as the operational requirement had been endorsed by all parts of MOD and here was a financial civil servant, with no equipment or military expertise, querying the need. I was rather worried about talking to the official as normally it is the financiers in the PE who have exclusive contact with Treasury because the military and the scientists are considered either too verbally incompetent or too politically naive to take on such a delicate responsibility.

In this case the PE principal had allowed me to speak direct, not because (as I first thought) I was rather an expert on operational requirements but because she was away for the day. I invited the Treasury official to my office where I was asked all sorts of questions on the operational use of the equipment. 'You see, we have to make sure that the taxpayers are getting value for money.' How could I not agree with that, but how on earth was the official achieving it? With little or no knowledge of military operations or equipment usage, my answers could hardly have been evaluated. My answers, as it happened, were truthful but I could have lied myself stupid and would not have been detected. The meeting was concluded with the statement that the Treasury was now happy with the operational need. A great big 'Tick-in-the-Box'. I do not blame the official for following procedures, but there must be something wrong with a system that depends on procedures that achieve nothing but a waste of several people's time.

This, of course, is not an isolated example. Large numbers of people spend a lot of their time and that of others scrutinising proposed expenditure without any real knowledge of what they are scrutinising. Not only scrutinising, but often insisting on change, on unsuitable solutions, on delay, or on yet more study. It is inefficient and ineffective and is codified in my Third Law of Equipment Procurement:

Despite increasing numbers and power of financial scrutineers, no effective scrutiny ever takes place.

You will meet my First, Second and Fourth Laws of Equipment Procurement in Chapter Seven. All this ineffective scrutiny runs counter to the government's much-trumpeted New Management Strategy (NMS) which seeks to reduce just such interference, and to delegate responsibility and authority to the lowest practical level. Surely no-one can seriously argue against such an objective. To all those with whom I worked it is plain common sense and long overdue.

The key is delegation of responsibility and authority. Both, not one or the other. And authority includes financial authority. Once both are delegated, the holder of both becomes accountable. He can make decisions without needing to find consensus amongst a host of peers, many of whom currently hold a veto. He can get on with the job and everything becomes more efficient, less painstakingly slow and cheaper. Why then is NMS not being pursued in large parts of MOD, particularly in the area I know so well, procurement? The defendants (of which there are plenty) say, give it time to work its way through a very complex system; it cannot be achieved overnight. Perhaps not, but NMS became a high-level policy objective more than five years ago. Since then NMS has been sidelined in key Defence Costs Studies, as we shall see later. Let one good example of the 'new thinking' suffice.

In 1992 most of the numerous research and development establishments were amalgamated to form the Defence Research Agency, and the responsibility for directing the applied research programme was taken from the scientists and given to the military. This was a very good move (very many scientists will now agree with this although few did at the time). Very clear letters of delegation were passed down from the Chief of Defence Procurement to the lowest delegated level, in some cases colonel or grade 6. Individuals were made responsible for directing a programme of research which met their needs at an affordable price. If the Defence Research Agency failed to produce acceptable deliveries on time, they were to withhold payment. So far, so good. But what payment?

Under the original Terms of Business Agreement or TOBA, the Defence Research Agency was to be paid by its military customer under three headings: progress payments as the work was done, milestone payments against satisfactory deliverables and profit. It was further agreed outside the Terms of Business Agreement that 80 per cent would be paid as programme payments, ten per cent as profit, ten per cent on milestone deliverables. Furthermore, costs agreed at the start would actually be cost-plus rather than fixed. If the customer refused to sign off deliverables as acceptable or refused to agree that profit has been earned, these would still be paid in full at the end of the year. As to the progress payments which totalled 80 per cent of all payments, these would be billed and paid without the customer having sight of, let alone any control over them.

This all adds up to the following: the Defence Research Agency could well finish the year being paid for a particular package of work, say 120 per cent of what was agreed originally, whether or not they had produced any acceptable deliverables. I am not suggesting that this is a regular occurrence as the Defence Research Agency's record on deliverables over the last two years or so has been pretty good; but it has happened and could well happen again or could even increase in frequency. Put starkly, I am not sure that many people would agree that the applied research military customer has been given the tools to discharge his extensive delegated responsibility. Some will claim that progress is being made with introducing greater flexibility into the arrangements, but the fact remains that the Defence Research Agency is still paid for effort, not achievement. Extensive effort is being made to achieve the right scientific research programme, but very little to achieve quality in the end deliverables. Such arrangements throw an unfair onus on individuals in MOD and the Defence Research Agency to make things work without relying on officially established principles or indeed by circumnavigating such principles. Furthermore, this goes largely unrecognised. I tried but was unable to persuade senior officers and officials that there is a problem; not surprisingly perhaps, as the issue is at the heart of the overall problem. Delegation seems to be fine as long as it does not include financial delegation. Yet financial delegation is essential to efficient decision-making and to proper accountability.

Financial delegation is anathema to the Treasury, which insists on vetting all equipment expenditure except for the very small projects. Unless this changes, financial delegation is a non-starter. However, in October 1994, the Treasury announced a cut of 30 per cent in its senior staff in an attempt to make itself more efficient. The Treasury's Permanent Secretary is reported as saying that his officials spend too much time second-guessing spending departments and that instead they should adopt a more strategic approach, handing out global budgets to departments and allowing these departments to determine how that money should be spent. If this happens, proper financial delegation within MOD would become a possibility, but not necessarily a probability. What are the chances? Low, I judge, from the chorus of 'pigs might fly' from all around me.

I mentioned earlier the subject of working practices. Given that there is no real accountability, that no significant decision can be made in procurement without the agreement of large numbers of people who can all block progress, and that much committee work with its tendency towards compromise decisions is necessary, the effort involved in making progress is already high. Add to this the absurdly frequent but ineffective scrutiny and it is higher still. It would make sense to ensure that working practices do not add to this effort and that everything is done to reduce it.

Certainly each time MOD has been reduced during the last 15 years or so, streamlining of working practices has been a constant cry: in 1981 when Army manpower in MOD was cut by 27 per cent, in 1991 during Options for Change, and in 1994 in the wake of the Defence Costs Study. To quote from *Focus*, the house journal of MOD:

> *The Defence Costs Study found that we are still too bureaucratic, paper dominated, hierarchical and over-inclined to seek to make decisions by consensus ... Similar recommendations were made following the Prospect Headquarters review but ... the same old ways of doing things continued.*

The Prospect Study referred to in this article was the exercise to reduce MOD headquarters in line with the reduction in the Services after the fall of Communism. Or roughly in line: 20 per cent was the target which hardly compares well with the 42 per cent reduction in the Royal Armoured Corps, the 27 per cent reduction in the Royal Artillery or the overall 25 per cent reduction in the Army. Nevertheless, 20 per cent reduction was sought. The study acknowledged that working practices must be streamlined: that delegation be made to lower levels, that initiative be rewarded, that oral briefings rather than written be the norm, that paperwork be reduced, that levels of management be decreased in number, that organisations be made more flexible and so on. I saw little change. That there has indeed been little change was emphasised by the Defence Costs Study which noted that the success of the streamlined and reduced head office would be critically dependent on the adoption of new working and management practices.

Another study was set up and I was one of 2,000 to receive a questionnaire. I replied in detail and at length, suggesting that those running the study might like to discuss my views. I heard nothing. Yet I believe my views were worth considering, not only because of my long MOD experience but because my views coincided exactly with the views of so many others. But as yet there have been no clear proposals, let alone decisions, to introduce streamlined practices that actually work. Let us look at some of the problems.

The first major issue to bear on working efficiency is rustication or dispersion. When I was in a Procurement Executive post in 1979, a move to Cardiff was imminent and individuals were already inspecting their new offices. Whether anyone had really considered how we were to work efficiently at a distance of 150 miles from many whom we needed to see on a daily basis I do not know. But I did not have to wonder for long, as the move was cancelled abruptly with a change of government. Whether this was a positive government decision or a dawning realisation that many of the top civilians would not leave London but disappear into the private sector with a massive income increase I do not know – clearly you can recruit clerical staff easily in Cardiff, but equally clearly you cannot recruit large numbers of experienced deputy under-secretaries in Cardiff (or anywhere else for that matter, not even in London).

So MOD headquarters remained spread across 20 buildings in London. In the 1980s there were fanciful notions of moving to the Docklands or even, after Thatcher's destruction of Ken Livingstone's Greater London Council, into County Hall, constructing a tunnel under the Thames to link it with the Main Building. Both these suggestions had great strengths: near colocation and a major improvement in work efficiency. Neither came to anything as London rents and rates continued to increase faster than elsewhere. To take advantage of this financially, a move out of London again became the aim. Not for those in the MOD Main Building heartland who could not countenance dashes to London by BR or BA to meet and discuss matters with those remaining (or perhaps could not countenance leaving the attractions of London with its clubs and part-time honorary posts), but for the hoi polloi, such as the Procurement Executive, the Military Secretary and many of the military operational branches. The fact that they needed to work closely with those who stayed in London was ignored or glossed over. 'Good trains from Bristol, you know', 'The Glasgow Shuttle is really very convenient.' For others you understand. After all, someone had to be inconvenienced if we were to make such massive financial savings.

The Procurement Executive is now concentrated at Abbey Wood near Bristol in a brand new, purpose-built complex on a green field site with, in the future, a BR station alongside. Advantages are claimed. Not financial benefits (the collapse of London rent and rates levels has torpedoed that argument), but of efficiency now that they are all together rather than spread across London. As Dr Malcolm McIntosh, then Chief of Defence Procurement (CDP), said in an interview with

Preview, the journal of the MOD Procurement Executive:

> *I have never had any second thoughts about co-location being the right decision ... my contact [now] is necessarily limited ... because of the physical difficulty of getting around all the sites that we have ... Abbey Wood will allow a much less constrained CDP than is possible at present. Instead of having all the briefings in my Main Building office, it will be easier to ... go to where the work is being done. It will be no effort for the CDP to get out of his office and go to a local briefing.*[4]

There is no doubt at all that the new complex is well-designed and a delight to work in. As John Gulvin put it: 'There is no rule which says that if you build a new building for civil servants it has to be unattractive.'[5] But has anyone who is connected with the decision (and it was looked at anew, allegedly both in depth and in objectivity, during the Defence Costs Study) considered the impact on those below CDP and his most senior managers, who have to work very closely with others back in London? Previously those in Operational Requirements, responsible for providing the user field expertise, had day-to-day contact with their opposite numbers in the Procurement Executive. With the reducing proportion of military officers in the Procurement Executive, these contacts become even more important, more frequent and more demanding. Without this contact, there will be an increased potential for Nimrod-type disasters. The decision to move to Abbey Wood was conceived as a financial expedient, and when that fell through as a demonstrable reason the decision was justified on internal management grounds. This of course is how major equipment decisions are now made. Little consideration is given to the end deliverable. Let us be quite clear, the move to Abbey Wood has the potential for disaster for Army equipment procurement.

Paperwork is perhaps the next issue to look at. In the world of procurement, leaving aside the forests of trivia that daily clog in-trays, this means the major submissions to committees, including the staff targets and staff requirements which detail exactly what an equipment must be capable of (from vehicle acceleration rates across country to the effects of its armament on the enemy, from its vulnerability to enemy firepower, electronic and chemical attack to its lifetime reliability), all in unambiguous English, against which the final design can be assessed. This is quite a challenge but must be done accurately, for this is the document against which will be written the technical specification, the basis for the contract with industry. Get the staff requirement wrong and you will rue it later in no uncertain terms.

Despite this, it is the accompanying 'supporting' committee paper which gets all the scrutiny and few people bother with the more important document. But they bother with the 'supporting' paper alright. Between 1985 and 1991, it was produced jointly by the user focus (Operational Requirements) and the Procurement Executive. It was supposed to pass through three drafts, each circulated at branch, director and director general level before the final paper was agreed by the 3- or 4-star protagonists for forwarding to the committee. The scrutineers fell on successive drafts like wolves and many appeared to think that their 'comments for considera-tion' – a euphemism for 'I will not allow this to progress any further until you include every single point I make' – had to be extensive to justify their existence. Not surprising, perhaps, as some of these people had little justification for existence. This led to repeated circulations at each level. No longer one, not even two or three or four. The submission on the AS-90 howitzer, which was really very straightfor-ward, went through ten separate drafts at the director general (2-star) level alone, almost all necessary to incorporate individual comments which increased with each draft. At the time I noted that often amendments to fundamental issues were made at one level of circulation which were at variance with what had been assumed to be correct from the comments (or lack of them) at the previous level, creating the impression that senior officers/civil servants had not been briefed in sufficient depth even when likely areas of debate could have been identified by their staffs in early drafts.

In 1991, the Prospect Study recommended a pilot study into a 'dossier' system for submission to the new Equipment Approvals Committee which was to replace the Equipment Procurement Committee. One submission from each Service was to be by way of the 'dossier' system to test it out. The selected Army project was to be the Chieftain replacement or Challenger 2 tank project – a good choice as it was about to get under way and was a large and high-profile project. There was one snag. By the time it was to be finished and the 'dossier' system evaluated, neither of my staff – the co-ordinator/chairman of the working group, nor the secretary – would still be in post. As a director I decided that I would have to attend working group meetings so that someone in Operational Requirements, which was leading, could make a sensible assessment of the new procedures. Once through the Equipment Approvals Committee, I sat back and marshalled my ideas ready for the request for my views. Nothing happened. Eventually I asked around and found that the system had been assessed and recommended for adoption without change. It appeared that during my absence on a two-day international meeting my comments had been requested, but a delay of two days was not considered acceptable. Much better of course to go ahead without views as this could complicate things with facts!

This was unfortunate as the 'dossier' system, like so many good ideas, has strengths as well as weaknesses. The strength is that there is only one formal circu-lation, worlds away from the ten drafts at director general level of the AS-90 paper in 1989. Of course this does not stop unofficial circulation at lower levels, but is a major step in the right direction. The main weakness is that it has created a con-sensus culture working group, which is officially what we are trying to get rid of. Instead of one or two authors who could ignore comments, there are now five authors and it is up to the chairman of the working group to obtain consensus on the adoption or otherwise of the comments received or he cannot go forward to a formal circulation. And consensus not only from those five authors, but from a growing band of scrutineers who are descending on the working group to have their pound of flesh. While the formal circulation of papers has been reduced drastically, the informal paperwork and consensus committee work has increased. Although the advantages are fast being eroded, it is overall still an improvement; but it could have been so much better with a little thought. Jumping to conclusions at the end, or often well before the end, of a pilot study is a favourite game in MOD. As I said, facts get in the way of decisions – life is much easier without them.

Currently all submissions have to be made in the 'dossier' format unless the circumstances are such that a short three-page note will suffice – this is not often, although common sense would make it more frequent than it is. A full dossier goes into everything in detail. Are we so inflexible that there is nothing in between? Inflexibility is of course an MOD hobby.

The Prospect Study concluded that oral rather than written briefings should become more frequent. There are times when a large written brief is necessary, even if it only contains the necessary papers for discussion at a meeting. But too many senior officers and officials call for written briefs without thinking through what exactly is required. The heights of absurdity reached can perhaps be illustrated by a call for a brief by a senior officer before he was to meet an industrial acquaintance for a general chat over a pub lunch – you cannot discuss classified business in a pub! Or a minister's private secretary who called for a brief, at a moment's notice, on 'armoured vehicles'. Which aspects did he want covered?' 'Oh ... everything!'

At the MOD debrief of the Defence Costs Study the subject of written briefs was raised. All the right words were said but the effect was torpedoed by another on the platform who observed that he 'felt comfortable with big, fat briefs'. The call for 'big, fat briefs' often follows a thought in the bath, or a lunch with someone with an axe to grind. Often, but to be fair not always, these are ideas that have already been discussed and for many good reasons rejected at a lower level, sometimes many times. It should therefore be easy to convince the man that it should not be pursued. But it is not. He may have given some verbal commitment to someone about following it up and he now wants a way out. This often leads to prolonged discussion at high level and fudged decisions, not always very sensible ones. It is often referred to as 'reinventing the wheel', but more often it falls under the category of 'proposing the replacement of a circular wheel by a square wheel'. No-one in the high-level, rather cosy world in MOD likes to speak bluntly – it is not regarded as 'helpful', it does not help to 'make the wheels go round', it is seen as 'arrogant' to believe you are right. As a result ridiculous suggestions are considered, evaluated, studied and in the process obtain such a momentum that the idea can survive for years; it might even become policy.

One issue that has been roundly condemned is the number of management layers. If inflexibility is adhered to, progress is slowed disastrously. As a result, it is becoming fashionable to go for 'flat' structures. In reality this means that in the extreme no-one knows what is going on. Is this the reality of the Defence Research Agency's latest 'flat' structure? While it is wrong to have to work rigidly through numerous levels to get a decision, a flexible hierarchical structure can reduce this to two or three, even for the biggest decision. The reality is that we must have a balance between depth and width. Managers must not be given too much width or they cannot effectively get to grips with their responsibilities, but neither should they have so little width that they micro-manage their subordinates. Both in the Army and in MOD, a well-tried size is three or four immediate subordinates each running his own area or group. Many more and the manager gets out of touch, less and he can only micro-manage, unless he has the strength of character to play golf twice a week. But then the financiers would not be persuaded by the cost-effectiveness of his post.

Flexibility is required. This means that everyone must let go once the subject has ascended above their level. None of the mentality that was so evident in the old regimental 'administrative inspections' as a general strode round a prearranged route, followed by a crocodile of his staff, officers and regimental commanders at all levels. The desk officer is the continuity person and keeps all informed. Hierarchical or flat structures are not the argument; flexible working practices within a hierarchical structure are.

It can go too far the other way. I was summoned to a meeting in the Minister's office on a subject which was being led by others. I had assumed I was there to add a little user reality (or 'tone', as others might put it) and that others would lead. Foolishly I did not check in advance. I was ushered into the meeting between the Minister and his German opposite number which was in full flow. The subject under discussion was helicopters, which was not one of mine. I sat back. I was obviously the first to arrive for the next item, I thought, and waited for the others. No-one else came. The Minister, who was in full command of the helicopter issues, then drew the discussion to a close and said, 'And now Brigadier Kincaid will tell you all about armoured vehicles.'

I mentioned earlier that administrative man is by nature an empire builder. To increase your empire and, just as importantly, to defend your empire against the depredation of others, you must have the latest information, you must be in on the act. In C. P. Snow's novel *Corridors of Power*, the old Minister, Thomas Bevill, believes that the first rule of politics is: 'Always be on the spot. Never go away. Never be too proud to be present.'[6] Never go away. Always be on the spot. That is to say, make sure you are always at any meeting where you might be damaged. Later I will cover a particularly damaging decision which was taken in my absence, possibly because I was known to be opposed. Another example of this wish to be in on the act was the one-time Armour/Anti-Armour Sub-Committee. When I took over as a director I became its chairman. I arrived at my first meeting to find the huge main conference room in the Main Building full of all sorts of people. The meeting was a disaster. Everyone wanted to have the floor at some stage to prove the need for their attendance; some wanted to run a seminar on tiny details. At the end, I said that I would reorganise the committee and would reduce it drastically. There were uneasy murmurs. I then instructed the secretary to chop attendance for the next meeting down to 15, certainly no more than 20, and to inform everyone. The resultant storm was interesting. Almost every individual of the 100 or so that had been at the earlier meeting made a case for their attendance and the basis, often unwritten but plain nevertheless, was the need to be there, not the wish to contribute. I was intransigent and many were angry. Inevitably the new committee grew slightly, but never to more than 25, and it soon began to make progress which would have been impossible without the change.

Never go away, never be excluded, always comment on papers whether you have something to say or not. These are the attitudes which lead to so much paper and so little output.

Output – a very fashionable demand these days. How do we measure it? With difficulty, is the answer. It is in fact supremely easy to measure the output of one procurement branch, but supremely difficult to allocate responsibility for shortfall if there is no real accountability as I have mentioned before. It is impossible to measure the output of many other branches, particularly of those which are primarily responsible for scrutiny for they have no obvious output. Nevertheless the enthusiasts march on, devising overarching strategies, policy papers, management plans with management objectives to meet, time sheets and so on to inflict on those who do the real work. Are they useful? No, not overall, but it gives those many, rather nebulous 'policy', 'plans' and 'secretariat' branches something on paper to measure their own output. This seems to me to be highly artificial. Not only that, it can be damaging as processes at a lower level are not often understood fully by the management planners. It can be damaging, too, as decisions are more frequently being taken not only for financial expediency reasons but on 'management' grounds.

One example will suffice. A new munition was in production when one munition in a batch behaved in an extremely odd way, falling some way behind the firing point. Clearly the reason needed to be identified quickly, a solution found and a 'fix' implemented before the Army could take delivery and declare the munition 'in service with the British Army'. But this in-service date was a 'management objective' in the Procurement Executive and I was horrified to find myself under pressure to ignore the problem and accept deliveries, to brush under the carpet considerable safety, financial and industrial implications for the achievement on time of a 'management milestone'. How silly will we get?

So where does all this scrutiny, this bureaucracy, this paperwork, these management initiatives get us? Do they really safeguard public money by ensuring we reach the right decisions every time, even if the huge delays involved cause greater expenditure? Are we now confident of avoiding more wasteful decisions like those in the past on TSR-2 and Nimrod? For this is the real test. We must safeguard public money and if we build in safeguards which push up costs, those safeguards must be effective. If they are not, then it would make more sense to abandon them and pay top salaries to the best people to do it themselves without scrutiny. We have a huge bureaucracy and time-wasting procedures. With what product? In the next chapter I shall look at a few recent decisions.

INTERLUDE TWO
A Day at Work

&

I threw back the bedclothes, swung my legs over the side of the bed and ... fell flat on my back on the floor. I do not usually misjudge my first action of the day quite so spectacularly – was it an omen? I glanced at the MOD calendar on the wall and saw that it was 339 January; an earlier LTC savings measure had led to the rationalisation of the traditional calendar, allowing only one month of 365 days. After a protracted battle at very high level, it had been agreed that the single month would be called January, rather than February (difficult to spell), March (with its infantry undertones), April, May or June (all too sexist), July or August (too imperial). Naturally the last four months were unsuitable for the new single month setup. There was some discussion over new names such as Challenger, Rapier and Warrior but these only opened up horrendous cap-badge warfare. When everyone was on the point of bleeding to death, a proposal to use January met with swift approval; its origin in Janus who was able to look both ways at once appeared to be fairly representative of MOD and there was only insignificant opposition from certain backward-looking quarters. Discussion on arrangements for leap years followed but it was amicably decided to commission a 2-star working group to report next year. Being a very backward fellow, I translated the new date into early December.

The newspaper had arrived when I got downstairs and I turned immediately to the sports pages to see whether England's top cricketers had managed to build on their wholly improbable first innings lead at Brisbane. I noted with satisfaction that the country's premier players had mustered a paltry 79 before they were all out; I felt the warm glow of I-told-you-so as the Chairman of Selectors had refused to consider my contention that I should form an integral part of the England attack and had been unnecessarily rude about my IQ and ancestry.

I arrived at our local British Rail station in the pouring rain – just what was wanted by gardens, sports fields, farmers, pessimists and wet blankets after so many dry seasons, but this happy thought was obliterated by the blank space on the cancellation board. 'Another boring routine journey', I thought as I gloomily watched the rain. At length there came an announcement. We do not go in for platform announcements generally, believing it much better not to know what is in store and to pick your way mentally blindfolded through the London suburbs, but an announcement there was. It did not enlighten anyone much as it was almost unintelligible. However, as it was bad news, it was repeated three times in a gleeful tone so we were able to make it out: 'The 07.12 ex-Farnham train is running approximately 41 minutes late.' I liked the 'approximately 41' bit. This was better! Which was the 07.12 ex-Farnham train? How did it relate to trains that might arrive at this platform? Were other trains delayed, or could I expect to catch an earlier train later? When might I now arrive at Waterloo? Would my whole day go delightfully pear-shaped?

These thoughts were smartly nipped in the bud by a further thrice-repeated announcement: 'That last message re the 07.12 ex-Farnham train does not refer to any of the next few trains which are all running on time.' Not strictly true as the next one was already several minutes overdue, but I was willing to stretch a point. 'What a pity', I observed to my neighbour, 'another boring journey.' 'Huh!' he replied, burying himself deeper in the financial pages; clearly one of those boring people who never vary their travel arrangements and communicate their disgust when their timetable is disrupted by puffing loudly and repeatedly through pursed lips. The non-stop to Waterloo drew in, full. I got on together with the rest of the platform and enjoyed closer companionship than normal: Close Encounters of the sordid kind, you might say.

At Waterloo it was still pouring, so I queued for a bus. Clearly no 507 had found Waterloo of late as the line of hopeful customers straggled all the way up the road and right across the station concourse. Nothing happened. This gave me a splendid opportunity to observe the activity around me as well as all those engaged in doing nothing at all, providing me with much valuable material for my forthcoming book on *The British Bus Queue – Is It Alive?* I am hoping that the snappy subtitle will send the sales soaring.

The queue continued to lengthen and I began to wonder where the tail might wind next. Through W H Smith's, perhaps, or up to the Ladies? Still nothing happened and I wondered why the AA did not sign Waterloo properly for poor 507 bus drivers whom I imagined lost in a vast metropolis, much like the Orly–Charles de Gaulle Paris airport shuttle-bus driver who had me on board once for several hours. Nothing happened for a long time and then three came along all at once – just like an elephant giving birth to triplets. I just managed to squeeze onto the last to enjoy more close encounters – odours of garlic and rotting teeth, stale perfume and decomposing armpits – a veritable cocktail of heady scents. The close encounters turned from sordid to painful with a stiletto heel on my bunion, a breathtaking elbow in my breakfast and a poke in the eye from an umbrella with a will of its own. An almost middle-aged lady regaled us with her views on her mentally retarded, slave-driving, odious boss whom she suspected of harbouring latent sexual harassment tendencies. She got off at my stop but I could not remember seeing her before.

I waltzed into my office with all the fervour of a wet Monday morning, hardly able to wait a moment longer to rectify last Friday's unfinished cockups. Sadly, none was immediate, at least until the first phone call of the week which pointed out an incorrect deadline – not Friday next but this morning. Good! That'll stimulate enthusiasm, concentrate the mind, repel boredom, I thought. I looked at the task but found it far from clear; what was the baseline, what was the question? Never mind, give it to the desk officers with some obfuscatory rhetoric and leave the building. Unfortunately I could not shirk the challenge like that as half of them were away at meetings in exotic venues such as Chorley and Feltham, and the others were wasting their time in Brussels or Paris. I would have to do it myself.

I took a deep breath, sat in front of the computer and composed. I had recently been given a brand new machine and was being dragged kicking and screaming into the 20th century, although I am not sure why when all the rest of the office machinery and procedures were Dickensian; you know, quill biros and bent paperclips, at least when there is no moratorium on such purchases, normally between April and March. I was still a novice at this computer business, but I did the startup procedures (the computer's – I would do mine later). The cursor winked at me sarcastically; my mind went blank. After a cup of coffee, I managed to type a couple of pages of nonsense. Having mentally congratulated myself, I noticed with slowly dawning horror that it was all in bold type and underlined. I had not noticed this before, being a one-fingered typist who has to watch the keys rather than the screen. I wondered whether anyone else would notice – would anyone read it? Perhaps someone would. I tried to take out the bold and underlining but deleted the whole text by mistake and had to start all over again. This time I shut and locked the door; someone had previously stuck a facetious notice on it indicating that my office was the typing pool – I still had the tatters of my pride. I progressed slowly, correcting all over the place, losing 'footers', gaining strange consonants, getting one margin straight only to entangle another like Spaghetti Junction, finding unwanted spaces in text that had earlier been exemplary and finally watching my signature block slide mysteriously off the bottom of the page. I gauped at the wonders of modern science.

I tottered out to lunch. Well, to what is recognised as lunch in my building. We do not have a kiosk; neither can we afford to lunch regularly in the local hostelries as we are not heirs to the family millions nor directors of Daddy's business, just fairly ordinary peasants. So we normally nip round the corner to Frederico's for a take-away sandwich, creep back to the office and use our imagination to match our dreams. I stood in the rain at the back of a straggly queue with fellow peasants from the Department of the Environment. The rain ran down my neck. There had been a spate of letters in *The Times* forecasting a blazing summer from someone who had observed that the frog spawn was upside-down and nuts had been plentiful. I pondered on the menu. Decisions, decisions! What to choose? After much cogitation, I plumped for a salad bap (OK for the waistline) and a hot meat pie (the opposite). At least it meant that I could put off the looming decision on a diet.

I arrived back at the office. No-one had rung all morning, but I go out for a moment and the whole world wants me. Ring the general, call the MA to the admiral, God will ring back in ten minutes; plus assorted messages from various lesser mortals. I ate my lunch and waited for God to ring, but he didn't.

Christopher strolled in. He is a nice lad but has a nasty tendency to think for himself which I have not managed to dislodge yet. He will get himself into trouble if I do not succeed soon. 'Hello!' I said, 'Had a good meeting?' I could not for the life of me remember where he had been but I thought that was a safe enough question. It was. 'No,' he replied, 'I arrived at Nottingham only to find they had moved it to Chorley and there was no way I was going to get there in time, even for the end of the meeting. So I came back here having wasted almost a whole day!' I could see he was annoyed and I tried to cheer him up: 'Never mind, it could have been worse: you might have had to make a decision.' He laughed – he thought I was joking. As I said, he was going to get himself into the mire sometime. He sauntered out.

A gentleman from the Office of Mismanagement and Bureaucracy rang, wanting to know the implications of postponing one of my most important programmes by several years. I tried to get rid of him with a holding reply but he needed an answer, as usual by yesterday. I then fobbed him off with fantasy and he rang off satisfied. Clever people in the Office of Mismanagement and Bureaucracy, so they tell me. I must ask them sometime why, when decision-making by the toss of a coin gives 50 per cent correct answers, MOD gets it wrong 97 per cent of the time (if you think it is more often than this, you are a cynic). Their answer would probably be delightfully complicated and centre around fiscal policy, the City and Peru, the Mickey Mouse accounting of the Treasury which assumes that the longer you postpone decisions the cheaper everything becomes, and the fact that Easter Day fell on a Sunday in 1962. As I said, clever people.

Can the same be said for the average Staff Officer Grade 2 in Airy Plans? 'I agree with the Office of Mismanagement and Bureaucracy – we know it makes sense!' An airy wave of the LTC wand, and, hey presto, it all vanishes. 'I'm sure you will understand that no system is perfect, even if we are!' says our Stiff Officer.

I read a letter from some obscure Procurement Expletive branch, apologising for missing my deadline and stating that their comments would be produced after the decision on a more important project was made. But as this other project is an armoured vehicle, it is not likely to be resolved soon; indeed, I suspect we are only in the first quarter of the match between the Office of Mismanagement and Bureaucracy and the Royal Armoured Corpse. On the one hand those with degrees from acceptable universities, and on the other those without degrees from an acceptable background. Neither can afford to lose this particular match, so it will probably eventually end in a low-scoring draw. The amount of paper produced would rival that in the Jarndyce vs. Jarndyce case in Dickens' *Bleak House*, which finished only when the money finally ran out. The scientists of course think they are refereeing the contest, but as they only have useful degrees from unacceptable universities they are totally ignored by both sides and cast into outer darkness along with politicians, industrialists, tradesmen, felons, RAF officers and sundry other unsavoury human beings.

I continued with my computer letter, and by late afternoon I had produced a presentable answer to the riddle. I addressed it to DScience (Fiction) and copied it to Overrational Retirements, Militant Orations, Army Staff Beauties, Deaf OR, MOO Sic, AUS (pogroms), DIns and TARDE (FH). I had used more than one finger and despite failing to check the spelling of the distribution had taken more than three times as long as it would have taken in longhand. This was progress. I had proudly conquered modern technology ... or at least had scratched its powerful surface.

The rest of the day was dull routine, including the news that my two largest, most interesting and successful projects had been cut. Of course at my level we are often lost in the maze of facts and are quite unable to comprehend the wider fiction. Fortunately our masters are not so earthbound and their stratospheric wisdom keeps us on the straight and narrow. We may have spent hundreds of millions on development but we shall not be wasting more on fielding this equipment. How lucky we are as taxpayers that someone guards our pockets. The decision had been made in heaven and had been passed down from archangels to angels to monarchs to heroes to under-secretaries and only finally to mere peasants like me. I did nothing. I am good at that. Anyway, I have yet to see a really irreversible MOD decision; it is usually considered more prudent to let things drift until planning is so blighted that it collapses from sheer boredom. That way no-one has to make an actual decision; it is done for them.

I left the office for the exciting journey home. As I approached the bus stop, a 507 sailed past and disappeared at an unlikely speed into the night. I walked. At Waterloo I found utter chaos. A broken line and some recalcitrant points had disrupted rail traffic in the whole of southern England, perhaps in Scotland as well. A blank indicator board stared at me and at thousands of others. After a long wait came the announcement that the 20.42 would leave from platform 19. This was most novel. But did platform 19 still exist or was it now buried under the Channel Tunnel terminus? I found it still intact and there was our train ... or at least a train. I got on; I waited; and waited. The train slowly filled up. When it was full, people in large numbers continued to push their way in. I had another dose of close encounters, now at the day's end of the very sordid kind. No-one spoke until a gentleman, in pushing his way on, lost a shoe between train and platform which generated much mirth and camaraderie. After some rather inefficient poking around with umbrellas, the shoe was retrieved, everyone was thanked and the carriage slowly sank back into its usual torpor. We sat. Two French ladies giggled; no doubt they were used to the efficiencies of the SNCF and had never experienced a snarl-up at Waterloo before.

No announcements, no sign of official life. Still we sat. Ladies huffed, gentlemen puffed, others looked pointedly and repeatedly at their watches. Someone wanted to know why the toilet was locked, but failed to get either a satisfactory answer to the mystery or relief from her distress for fear of missing the train's departure. I assume she exercised her muscles. Then a judder, the train moved two yards and stopped. 'End of the line; all change!' shouted some wag. 'Is this train still going to Guildford?' asked an elderly lady. 'No dear, first stop Edinburgh,' sang out our wag. 'Thank you so much, I'm much relieved,' replied the lady. 'That's more than I am,' called out the desperate female. And then, in what seemed the middle of the night, the train pulled away and clattered over the points. The lights went out. The French ladies thought this hilarious and chattered away about the iniquities of the English, the inefficiency of British institutions and the total superiority of the French race. Everyone else slept.

In due course I alighted in a gale with raindrops stinging my face. 'What a day!' I thought as I strode home. 'But I suppose that it can only get better.' As if anything ever did!

CHAPTER SIX

Big Decisions and Sacred Cows

As soon as questions of will or decision or reason
or choice of action arise, human science is at a loss.
PROFESSOR NAOM CHOMSKY, TV INTERVIEW IN 1978

The fall of Communism took the West by surprise, particularly the speed at which it happened. To most, it was inconceivable until it took place. Six months before the fall of the Berlin Wall, a civilian friend of mine said, 'Do you think the two Germanys will ever be united?' He was surprised when I said nothing was more certain. 'You mean in 15 years or so?' 'No, in less than five.' Six months later, the two were in all but fact one. Far more accurate than my friend who worked in the City, I was still proven hopelessly wrong. The West was taken aback.

There were two immediate reactions in Whitehall. The first was the cry for a major peace dividend. 'Build hospitals not tanks', was the mood of the moment in the wake of those incredible scenes on and around the Wall in November/December 1989. This was an irresponsible reaction, but the media pressure and the clear benefit that substantial cuts in the defence budget would have for the ailing economy as a whole were difficult to resist. And the Treasury was not about to be resisted. Irresponsible? Certainly, for we had moved from the relative safety of a world clearly divided between the influence of two superpowers, operating under clear rules, to the unknown where revolution or war in many parts of the world might go unchecked, most dangerously perhaps in Eastern Europe and the former Soviet republics. Russia remained a hugely powerful military force and who was to say that there would not be an early return to hard-line Communist dictatorship and an overwhelming desire to interfere militarily in former Warsaw Pact states? While the threat of an invasion of Western Europe had been all but eliminated, Russian interference in Poland or Czechoslovakia might well have created extremely difficult circumstances for NATO. Today such fears may appear to have been groundless, but in 1990 nothing was certain, everything was new ground which might prove to be shifting sand.

Parts of MOD saw this quite clearly, but the Treasury turned a blind eye. The defence budget was to be reduced – and in the short term, too. Given this decision, MOD was commendably quick off the mark and in February 1990 set up its Options for Change project to identify the future size and shape of the country's armed forces. The problem was that no-one else was moving as quickly. Without similar deliberations in other NATO countries, there could be little useful debate in NATO and no common plan. Without a NATO plan, it was difficult to identify the main factors that must shape Britain's new Navy, Army and Air Force. There was little political guidance beyond the need to play a major part both in Europe and in NATO and to remain at the necessary level in Northern Ireland. On such flimsy ground, the required numbers of infantry battalions or artillery regiments were difficult to determine.

It is difficult to solve equations if the unknowns are too numerous. There were, however, two 'givens'. The first was the size of the reduced budget, or rather the size of the cut that was to be taken as a peace dividend. The second was the equipment programme which would have to continue because cancellation of major projects well into development or production under tight contracts was unlikely to save much and could in some cases cost more. But projects which were at a much earlier stage of development were scrutinised and many were placed on hold for potential savings. These two factors gave some sort of base to the planning, and the Army added two more: the regimental system was to remain undiluted and the corps level was to be retained. The thinking behind the latter was in my opinion sound, as once lost it would not easily be recovered. It was acknowledged, however, that this built in a degree of overstretch from the start. The immediate decision to keep alive the sacred cow of the regimental system is less easy to defend: it has undoubted strengths, but it is expensive in manpower and should at least have been examined more closely.

This great change, such as happens perhaps only once in anyone's working life, was a chance to gauge whether the MOD decision-making process worked efficiently. There was, of course, profound concern within all ranks of the three Services. This concern was heightened by the knowledge that a finance-led defence review was being carried out without any NATO or national doctrine for the 'brave new world' that was appearing. Morale was further damaged by the secrecy in which all this was happening. In an article in the *Financial Times* of 18 March 1991, David White wrote:

> *The review process was kept under tight control to avoid public arguments between the different Services. But keeping the armed forces in the dark began to threaten morale and in late July Mr. King announced the outline conclusions.*

This announcement deepened the gloom. The Army was to be cut by 25 per cent (compared with an average of 18 per cent for all three Services) and reduced from four armoured divisions to two. There was little more detail; the extent of, and plans for, redundancy, uppermost in many people's minds, were yet to be tackled and most future equipment projects remained on hold.

In 1981, Nott's defence review had targeted the Royal Navy, but within a year it was reprieved by the Falklands War. Within eight days of the Defence Secretary's announcement quoted above, Saddam Hussein marched into Kuwait and Britain responded by sending troops which amounted eventually to a small division of around 9,000 fighting men on the ground; with the necessary backup the force totalled 27,000. At the conclusion of the war, it was clear that

Britain's army will have cause to remember its participation in the war against Iraq. It may never do anything like it again. Current plans for defence cuts would, according to senior officers, make it impossible to mount the same operation two or three years from now. The Gulf crisis has brought home some of the implications of the defence cuts that the government announced last summer under the title Options for Change.[1]

Unlike the aftermath of the Falklands, when the Navy's surface fleet was reprieved, there was no such silver lining for the Army after the Gulf War. I am not sure why, but I suspect that the only clear factor was the financial one as firm assertions on future policy and doctrine were open to challenge by one and all. There was no proof that the cuts were too deep. Or was there no will? Or was the decision-making process in MOD utterly unsuited to the sort of decisions it was now being required to make? Alan Clark's view is typically forthright:

This happens the whole time. It's not just the slow balls-up of the 'Options' project, it's a hundred examples a week of waste, blinkers, vested interest, idleness and failure to put the country before narrow personal, regimental or sectarian considerations.[2]

For some time, the focus of likely operations remained Central Europe, albeit further to the east: East Germany and Poland rather than West Germany. And a different type of operation: no longer a defensive operation with limited counterattack but a much more offensive one. This called for new thinking. Would we need to change the balance of our forces, or our weapons? There were no quick answers for two reasons: there was no body within MOD to formulate either concepts or doctrine and crucially, given its popularity, scientific operational analysis lacked the model scenarios now most likely.

Once upon a time the Army had looked to the Directorate of Combat Development (Army) to produce a vision of the future battlefield but regrettably (because it was doing a good job the cynics would claim) it was replaced by a body, located out of London, called the Arms Executive (ARMEX). This was a failure. Then came Heseltine, and the Directorate of Defence Concepts was set up in the Central Staffs. Just what was wanted; or so we thought. But it was just what was not wanted in some quarters. If a draft concept paper appeared to undermine the requirement for a new aircraft, it was not long before the Chief of the Air Staff was tearing into it, if a tank, then the Chief of the General Staff, if a frigate, the Chief of the Naval Staff. The Services were still strong, but critically those in Defence Concepts were lacking in background, broad expertise and intellect. The qualities of a good military officer were just not enough to carve future concepts between, or indeed through, the sacred cows of the three Services. Before long, Defence Concepts had been moved, renamed and downgraded in its terms of reference. No longer was it to produce concepts for the future, it was to study 'force development'. The difference is not clear, but future concept papers were not to be its business. This inevitably happened just as the world was changing radically for the first time since 1948.

The lack of doctrine persuaded the Army to set up a Directorate of Land Warfare to provide exactly what had been missing since the disbandment of the Directorate of Combat Development in 1980 – doctrine for the future battlefield. This was a major step forward. Yet despite the claim that the top middle-ranking Army intellects were now concentrated at Upavon in Wiltshire, only slow progress was made. It was not until 1995 that any clear output suitable for guiding the equipment programme was produced and even this was of limited quality. Nevertheless it was a start. There was, however, a further problem: the Directorate of Land Warfare was an Army body reporting eventually to the Army Board. The output from such a body was not accepted in the post-Heseltine tri-Service ('purple') MOD until it had 'purple' endorsement. But there was no 'purple' body to endorse it, nor any 'purple' concept against which Army doctrine could be endorsed. Stalemate. The black hole at the centre of decision-making remained. It is now expected that the recently formed Permanent Joint Headquarters will fill the void. We shall see. I do not intend to bet on it.

This black hole is nothing new and in recent years it has been partially filled by scientific operational analysis. Military judgement is a dirty word in MOD as the scrutineers believe it to be biased by definition; but scientific operational analysis depends entirely on the input data and assumptions – get these wrong and the answer will be wrong. Even if they are right but have not been agreed, the study conclusions are likely to be pulled to pieces by those who do not like the answer it has produced. The trick is to ensure that the military and the scrutineers agree on the opening assumptions and the input data before the study starts and when the study is finished to carry out 'sensitivity analysis' by changing those assumptions and data that are open to argument to see whether any of them drive the result and if so, how.

Operational analysis, if done properly in this way, can produce excellent guidance for decision-making. In an earlier chapter I mentioned the saga of HVM and the air defence gun. It was fortunate for all concerned that the main operational analysis study was extremely well done or the arguments would never have been resolved. The so-called E5 study succeeded because of the painstaking way in which the initial assumptions and data were discussed in minute detail by a large body of experts, military and scientific, over a long period to ensure there were no weaknesses. Anything that was not clear-cut and fully agreed was noted for 'sensitivity analysis' at the end. The final result was clear, robust and readily accepted by all the important people; the others were easily sidelined, though not without a little grief.

The E5 study looked at the best solution for improving the army air-defence capability in 1st British Corps. This was a relatively low-level task and therefore fairly straightforward. As the subject gets wider, operational analysis becomes more difficult – assumptions and data increase quickly, probably on an exponential scale, and the range of experts required becomes far larger. One example was the Army's attempt in the mid-1980s to find out which of its anti-armour weapons were the most cost-effective so that it could reduce the overall equipment spend in the anti-armour area by deleting the least cost-effective weapons, and so take the pressure off its budget. I suspect it was also set up in the hope of showing the cost-effectiveness of the tank and the need for more tank regiments – perhaps funded at the expense not of Army weapons but of Naval and Air Force equipment.

Project Foresight was begun in 1984 and was followed by Project Foresight 2 and then by Project Foresight 2B – a logical progression. In my opinion it was pretty well done. I had some involvement with the indirect fire studies and felt that the overall study was on firm ground. There was just one weakness: it failed to conclude that the tank was more cost-effective than other anti-armour systems, the tank actually coming out very poorly overall. This is of course explained by the fact that the tank is not just an anti-armour weapon but the major component of any aggressive move. Not surprisingly, the result was seized on by those who were opposed to more investment in tanks. Not surprisingly, the study was buried by those who had commissioned it.

This was easy to do as, post-Heseltine, it was not a bi-Service study – the air anti-armour dimension was missing. The LIBRA study was consequently set up and got severely out of its depth, bogged down in a morass of recriminations over assumptions. Operational analysis at this level is difficult. Perhaps too difficult, for if you make sure that every single assumption and all input data are agreed by every expert, and allow enough time at the end for the necessary 'sensitivity analysis', the study will take so long that decisions will already have been made long before the study reports emerge, or the assumptions and data will have changed so significantly that the conclusions are meaningless. Yet if you take shortcuts, the study will never gain the confidence of those who must use the results.

My personal view is that high-level operational analysis is largely ineffective. I expressed this view at a high-level committee meeting which was debating a programme of studies to support Options for Change. I was particularly sceptical about the proposed timetable of about two years, and my conclusion was that there was no chance of useful results on such a time scale. The chairman was incensed, and I was not invited to attend that committee again. These high-level or 'overarching' linked studies, known as I19, I20 and I21, got going but the then Defence Operational Analysis Centre failed to involve outsiders or to clear assumptions and data with the advisory group, which was set up specially to do just that, and ploughed on in an attempt to meet the ridiculous timetable. There was no proper 'sensitivity analysis'. No surprise then, at least to me, when the study was buried under the highest tide of vitriol I have ever seen. For once in its history, MOD was united: the conclusions of I19, I20 and I21 were rejected. This was embarrassing for the scientists, one of whom seriously suggested accepting the bits he liked! Much work had gone into these studies and some parts were useful, but there was no real desire to extract those parts which rested on sure foundations. It did, however, give rise to further studies; but I remain sceptical about the probability of success.

The failure of such high-level studies is, in my opinion, almost preordained. Failure is made more certain by those who try and squeeze the time available to force answers they require in a time scale they want. If the person in charge of the studies is weak he will bow to this pressure in case he gets no more work, and will produce rubbish. This is a pity as good operational analysis is of outstanding value.

If high-level operational analysis is too difficult, if low-level operational analysis is ignored, and if we have no useful concepts or doctrine, how are decisions made? This is a very good question. The answer is that they are made in a variety of ways, not one of which is intellectually satisfying. Moreover, they are in effect made almost entirely at a low level – at least the successful ones!

This is nothing new; if we go back to 1982, near the beginning of my involvement in such matters and seemingly a lifetime away at the height of the Cold War, in the middle of NATO's three per cent defence budget increase every year in real terms and pre-Heseltine 'purple-isation', we see much the same thing. A good example was the selection of the frequency for the surveillance radar of the Rapier Field Standard C surface-to-air missile system. Field Standard C followed B2, which followed B1, which followed A – all highly logical. I ought to point out that Field Standard C is an almost entirely brand new equipment, is very efficient and at the time of writing is entering service with the Army and the Royal Air Force. But back in 1982 we were still sorting out the major parameters, and radar frequency was one of them. The Rapier project manager was one of the very few legendary characters in MOD procurement (most are thoroughly grey and forgotten pretty quickly). Colonel Ken Grantham-Wright sported long, untidy hair and a large moustache, claimed to have refused promotion to general, hated stuffed shirts and ignorant posers, was delightfully irreverent to one and all, and never stopped talking. It was rumoured that he ran his own business in Salisbury at the weekends and at night during the week, lived in a dilapidated mansion swarming with teenage kids and their friends and Bohemian *joie de vivre*. It was also purported that he had absolute control over his financial civil servants and that is certainly how it seemed. I was trying to extract some figures one day when I was told by one of the accountants that he could not oblige as all his papers were locked in the Colonel's cupboard and he was away all day!

Whether or not Ken had refused promotion I know not, but he did not court high-level support. He was summoned to appear before the Executive Committee of the Army Board to explain why he required quite so much money for the Rapier project. A special meeting was set up for the explanation. All assembled for a 2 p.m. start and the chairman introduced the subject and called on Ken for his presentation. No Grantham-Wright was present. The meeting was adjourned for ten minutes while military assistants rushed out to look for him. Twenty minutes passed, and in walked Ken, hair awry, pipe smoking like an ancient battleship, and arms full of vufoils and papers. He dumped the papers in front of the Vice-Chief of the General Staff with the words: 'And you're **** lucky that I'm only 20 minutes late considering the decrepit office machinery you give us to work with!', stalked up to the other end of the room, spread his vufoils all over one end of the table, obliterating the papers of several distinguished board members, and began. After 30 minutes of busy technical vufoils and masterly use of the technical language he said: 'Any questions?' He demonstrated his usual two ways of dealing with questions. If he judged the questioner to be important, he said: 'That's a very interesting point, but to answer it I must cover two other points first', and proceeded to dive into the most abstruse technical detail before suddenly saying, 'Does that answer your question?' to which the bemused questioner, who had not followed one word, could only say, 'Yes, thank you very much.' To those he judged as unintelligent or unimportant or to whom he had just taken a plain dislike, he said: 'Now I've been through all that and all these other gentlemen have got the point; do you really want me to waste their time by going through it again just for you?' It was devastating.

Ken was a very clever man. Returning to the saga of the surveillance radar frequency, I attended a presentation at what was then the Royal Aircraft Establishment at Farnborough for the results of a major study into this subject. The presentation was clear and the recommendation for D-band was clearly supported by the facts. At the end, Ken said: 'That's a load of b****; you've got it wrong!' When asked what exactly was wrong, he replied that the assumptions were wrong. 'But', said the study leader, 'You agreed the assumptions before we started.' 'No', Ken maintained, 'I could never have agreed to such nonsense.' 'But I have your signature here on the assumptions document.' 'I may have signed it', said the incorrigible Ken, 'but I never agreed it. Anyway they're wrong.' Whereupon he leapt to his feet and gave a masterly technical exposition as to why it should be J-band. Today the Rapier Field Standard C surveillance radar operates at J-band.

The reader will say that this was in the bad old days and that such decisions could not be made these days without copious scrutiny all the way up the chain. But it does happen all the time even now. The technical parameters and system design of a £10m radar, the detailed requirements for a £2bn programme or the exact content of the £500m research programme are never properly considered or discussed above director (brigadier) level, and most of this very important content will be decided at desk or at most assistant director level. And it is right that it should be as this is where the expertise lies. Even in the annual programming saga of the LTCs, 90 per cent or more of the decisions are made effectively at assistant director and colonel level or below. Again this is right and proper because at this level all aspects can be considered properly by those with access to, and time to consider, all the details.

This is an important point. Once decisions are placed in the hands of those without the necessary expertise, time and knowledge, things go wrong. And of course it is the big decisions which are, more and more, made by people without the necessary expertise, time and knowledge or are made for the wrong reasons, or are made for genuine reasons but cloaked for 'respectability' under a veneer of stately consideration by studies or consultants or committees. Let us consider a few such high-level decisions.

We have already noted the E5 study and the decision to buy the Short's HVM air defence missile system. It was a good decision, but I wonder if today such a decision might have been different or distorted by central programmers or accountants. Another project in which I was involved from beginning to end was the terminally guided warhead for the successful multiple launch rocket system (MLRS). The MLRS launcher and its basic bomblet warhead, which was deployed with such great success in the Gulf War by the British and American artilleries, started as an American project. Four European nations (United Kingdom, France, Germany and Italy) 'bought into' the project in the late stages of development and it was subsequently manufactured complete in both the United States and Europe. Four of the five MLRS nations (Italy was unable to find the funds to join) set up the joint development of a very high-technology MLRS munition capable of autonomously seeking, homing onto and destroying enemy tanks. It was an expensive project at the leading edge of technology. Although it took a year or two for the genuinely multinational industrial consortium to settle down, the project then made spectacular progress. The original development contract was signed in November 1984 but had to be rebased in January 1986 after new intelligence on future Soviet tanks was confirmed. Thereafter every technical and system challenge was met successfully with very little schedule slip and minimal cost increase. By 1992, the project was heading towards a full 'end-to-end' or launch-to-strike demonstration, when first the United States announced their intention to withdraw at the end of the penultimate stage of development in 1995 in favour of a national alternative programme (a decision since seen by many as a bad one), and then Germany for financial reasons in

the wake of the changes in Eastern Europe. The programme continued to a very successful 'end-to-end' test in which one round was fired, sub-munitions dispensed at the correct point, fins and wings deployed, correct flight altitude found, search radar activated, the target found, homed onto and struck, all activities controlled entirely by electronics and sensors within the sub-munition. A technical triumph for the nations and industries involved.

Shortly before this test, France had sought to continue the programme through the final development stage into production in conjunction with the United Kingdom. It would have been more expensive with only two participating nations, but not greatly so. In fact, by reducing quantities in line with the reduced Soviet threat, the UK share could have been contained within the financial provision made in the current LTC. A high-level decision to go ahead with a bi-national programme was clearly needed, but it seemed at the time to be a straightforward issue. The Army placed high priority on the munition, funding was available, the project was outstandingly successful and risk was low.

Regrettably, the funding had been removed from the Army and placed under the central programming staff for either the MLRS munition (known as MLRS III) or for the non-existent air force air-to-ground anti-tank missile known as SR(A) 1238. There was in fact enough funding for both systems in the quantities needed after the Cold War. But the central programmers were insistent that it was one or the other, not both, and that if fewer were required, half the funds could become a saving. Which was it to be? The highly successful MLRS III munition which existed as a largely proven system, to be fired from an outstandingly successful in-service launcher, or a drawing-board paper project which proposed to use some mature technology but, in system terms, was not even defined properly, in particular the key question of how the target was to be acquired by the aircraft before launch of the missile. There were other key uncertainties with SR(A) 1238. Additionally, there was little or no operational analysis to support it while MLRS III enjoyed the support of probably the greatest volume of operational analysis and wargaming ever to sustain a future equipment. In fact when I gave a presentation to the four-nation user working group on the UK studies over ten years, the other three nations were astounded by their range and depth and bemoaned the fact that their national studies were by comparison limited. They were simply amazed by the scientific and military evidence which we had assembled to prove the worth and sheer cost-effectiveness of MLRS III. I doubt if there will ever be anything similar to support a future project.

Nevertheless, a working group was set up to recommend the way ahead. It was generally understood that one of the two was for the chop, but officially the working group was to look at the options, including the possibility of having both. The working group consisted of about 20 people, of which only two were Army. Almost every influential post at 1-star level in MOD at that time happened to be filled by an Air Force officer and there must have been ten or twelve of them. The remainder were civil servants. The other Army officer was a member of the central programming staff and was in the process of stitching up a deal to ensure that the Army got the tanks it needed. He was effectively sidelined in the MLRS III/SR(A) 1238 working group. I was a lone voice and it was easy for the chairman to claim that my view was unsupported by the rest of the large group. Nevertheless I managed to keep things on an even keel without too strong a threat to MLRS III; after all I had extremely strong arguments on my side. But then I had to miss one meeting to attend an important international meeting on another project. When I came back I found that MLRS III had in effect been recommended for termination; in my absence it had been easy to arrive at a consensus. I recalled Snow's old Minister Thomas Bevill and his belief: 'Never go away.'

Was this a good way to make a very important decision on how to dispose of £1bn of taxpayers' money? Of course not. But do not think that this was how the decision was actually made, for it was not. Before even the first meeting of this working group took place, the decision had been made by a high-ranking member of the Central Staffs that, as RAF planes had ineffective weapons, the RAF must have SR(A) 1238. I would support that. What is less easy to understand is why this meant cancellation of MLRS III when there was funding available for both, when the Army placed MLRS III near the top of their priorities, and when MLRS III was one of only very few highly successful projects.

The working group was set up as a veneer of respectability for a snap decision by one senior officer on a spurious basis – not the fact that RAF aircraft needed a new weapon, which they clearly did – (incidentally, how does this escape committees time and again when aircraft projects are approved without satisfactory weapons?), but that he insisted on one or the other when both were needed, and the cost-effectiveness of each needed to be tested against many other weapons across the whole defence budget.

Another example of unsatisfactory decision-making was the new tank to replace the old and unsatisfactory Chieftains, only some of which had been replaced by the Challengers built originally for the Shah of Iran but taken by the British Army after the Shah's fall. Replacing the remaining Chieftains was urgent at the time I returned from the Procurement Executive to Operational Requirements in November 1987 and I was told the decision was imminent. I was not involved in any of the decision process but it seems that it was impossible to gain consensus amongst the growing number of people who could interfere officially. MOD was looking for value for money, but the political dimension could not be overlooked: did it make sense to buy overseas, thereby destroying UK industry's ability to manufacture tanks in the future? Combined with detailed evaluation of the competing tanks, and other factors such as interoperability with the smoothbore guns of our allies or intra-operability with the rifled guns of our Challengers, it was a complex decision, but not hugely so. Certainly not so complex as to keep putting it off. No decision had been made when the Wall fell, providing an excuse for yet more procrastination. By this time many Army officers felt they did not care which tank they got, as long as they got one quickly. Still the decision was postponed. In July 1994, the Secretary of State finally announced that the Army would get 259 Challenger 2 tanks. It had taken seven years to make this decision. The effort put into providing papers and briefs during that period was immense. If laid side to side I suspect they would have reached from Whitehall to Vickers in Leeds and back 259 times.

The real problem was that the tank is a virility symbol of the Army. Cold War comparisons of NATO and Warsaw Pact power were usually depicted by numbers of tanks, aircraft, ships and strategic missiles. All these are easily counted and placed on maps. Other things, even artillery and infantry vehicles, are less easily aggregated and carry little weight in the power analysis. Making decisions about such symbols is emotive, as is demonstrated by the recent debates over the Eurofighter aircraft.

Big decisions need clear thought within an agreed policy. We have no agreed policy, certainly not on equipment. Unbelievably, when the Equipment Policy Committee was restructured as the Equipment Approvals Committee, equipment policy was written out of the new terms of reference. When I queried this as an oversight, I was told it was deliberate. I could not believe it and said so. 'But', was the response, 'the superseded committee never made or even discussed equipment policy, so there's not much point in including it in the new terms of reference!' This is of course symptomatic of decision-making in MOD – ignore policy and let decisions happen.

Without a policy, clear thinking is difficult because everyone has a different base line. The financiers, of course, love this; it is difficult to argue a case against a cut or for more money without an agreed baseline. Without an equipment policy, big decisions will continue to be taken piecemeal and for the wrong reasons. Again, this is nothing new. In *The Blunted Sword*, Divine exposes the faulty logic and lack of clear policy thinking in equipment decisions of the 1960s: the large carrier and the aircraft P1127, P1154 and TSR-2.[3] Big decisions today suffer from a lack of clear thinking, a lack of an overall equipment policy and expediency.

Examples? How about the emotional defence of high-performance manned aircraft by the RAF. The RAF was the only Service in 1993 not to be investing in research into the capabilities of unmanned aircraft, which are not only in service with armies and air forces elsewhere, but which could carry out many RAF functions at a fraction of the cost in money and manpower. Ground-based air defence is a similar case. High-performance manned aircraft may be essential for some tasks but can the numbers be justified? Apart of course from the necessary air crew pyramid to give birth to Air Force Board members.

What about the surface fleet? At the time of Nott's review in 1980, no clear rationale emerged for surface units in general war, despite the huge sums of money spent on the defence of these ships from attack by sea and air. I remember a submariner telling me gleefully: 'There are two classes of ship: submarines and targets.' The

Falklands War may have clarified the issue somewhat, but have the numbers been justified? I suspect not.

Just to keep this chapter on a proper 'purple' footing: why has the Army allowed no proper debate over the regimental system? Is the cost and inefficiency in terms of manpower justified by increasing fighting power? Is this possible when units are mixed and matched in war? I do not know, but neither does anyone else as it has never been debated properly. It was a 'given' at the start of Options for Change, and a sacred cow during the Defence Costs Study (where no sacred cows were to be allowed).

Frigates, aircraft, tanks and the regimental system are all subjects that generate enormous emotion. The Navy, Army and Air Force Boards will fight tigerishly on behalf of them and civil servants know when to leave alone – particularly on subjects which are likely to bring ministers into conflict with large numbers of MPs in the Commons. Just dress up these emotional single-Service views in a 'purple' robe. Policy? Who wants policy to muddy big decisions? Making decisions is a risky business now that more and more accountability is demanded. The military are used to making important decisions as are, to a lesser extent, scientists. But administrative civil servants are not and seek increasingly to put them off or to allow others to produce 'unassailable' evidence so that they can slope their shoulders. In the last resort they depend on consultants. Simon Jenkins wrote in *The Times* in February 1995 on the subject of furnishing and decorating costs of official residences:

> *It is a growing habit of the Civil Service to duck accountability by delegating tough jobs to the private sector. £100,000 to describe a £380,000 decorating bill as too high and assign blame is inexcusable. In a more courageous age this job would have been done by a junior official in a week. We are not told which official authorised this grotesque sum, or if he is on 'performance-related' pay.*

Proper decision-making on difficult issues is becoming less and less likely.

That Tortoise a Lesson

੩**

Augustus was a prehistoric tortoise, born and bred,
    A soldier in the prime of life, so everybody said:
The troops he led in battle, which they'd regularly win,
Were lost in admiration for the thickness of his skin.

He'd joined the Tortoise Army, as his father had before,
    When still a teen-aged tortoise at the age of fifty-four,
His company Commander wrote 'Augustus should do well,
    Provided that he doesn't try to come out of his shell.'

He never did. Commissioned in the Tortoise Armoured Corps,
    Augustus rose to high command as war succeeded war.
'His shells are always loaded', was a legendary joke;
Another was 'One tortoise back, two up and bags of smoke.'

'The tortoise rules the battlefield', Augustus used to say,
    'An Army full of tortoises will always win the day.
We're mobile, well protected, and a set of healthy jaws
Can look so damned aggressive that the enemy withdraws!'

Accordingly, as time went by, Augustus topped the charts
    For intellectual brilliance in the military arts
And after every battle, he would lead his soldiers' cheers:
'The tortoise on the battlefield will last a thousand years!'

Tacticians should know better than to say such foolish things,
    For who can tell what challenges the unexpected brings?
It brought upon the tortoises a threat upon their heads
Which tore their cherished prehistoric principles to shreds ...

Augustus wasn't looking when the pterodactyls struck
And got him in the rear, which was a bit of rotten luck.
He tried to stroll for cover but attacking at the glide,
They turned Augustus turtle, which was most undignified.

The inversion of their leader took his soldiers by surprise;
They gathered round him helplessly with panic in their eyes.
'What now?' they asked Augustus and he answered with a groan;
'The ptime has come to ptrain some pterodactyls of our own!'

Recruiting pterodactyls was a simple thing to do
But learning how to use them was a bitter pill to chew.
It dawned on poor Augustus that his plans would come to nought
Unless he learned the principles of intimate support.

The very thing appalled him and it chilled him to the bone,
For hitherto the tortoises had always fought alone.
How could he grasp the intricate complexities of flight,
Apply them to his strategy and hope to get it right?

Collecting all the pamphlets he could find, he read them through,
But most of them were obsolete (and unamended too);
He'd ask one pterodactyl for its views, and in a trice
A dozen more would offer contradictory advice.

Alarmed by all this bickering, Augustus said 'Enough!
We've got to go to war again – I'll play it off the cuff.
Judicious application of the principles of war
Will defeat the opposition, as it's often done before.'

The battle was a shambles and the slaughter unconfined,
And all because Augustus couldn't quite make up his mind;
His pterodactyl squadrons were committed to the fight
Too late upon the left and far too early on the right.

Augustus lost that battle many million years ago
By dint of a mentality too ponderous and slow.
He never would have lost the war, if someone had been there
To co-ordinate resources on the ground and in the air.

The tortoise has survived today - a pacifistic strain -
But pterodactyls snuffed it and were never seen again.
It serves the pterodactyl right - the blame was partly his;
I'd like to find a moral but I don't know where it is!

Afternote: Although this was produced by a now extinct race, their Darwinian offshoot thinks that a degree of relevance can still be discerned, and wishes the Tortoise well in the development of its doctrine and equipment.

N.B. The author of this little homily, GRM, has unfortunately not been traced. A pity as I should like to acknowledge his authorship.

CHAPTER SEVEN
Intricacies of Equipment Procurement

MOD has finally woken up to the fact that for 30 years
the Defence Industry has been ripping off their customers.
AN ANONYMOUS INDUSTRIALIST[1]

A ddressing a Brassey's seminar in December 1993, John Weston, Chairman of British Aerospace Defence Limited, welcomed the Defence Costs Study, which had recently been announced in the House of Commons, with the following words:

> *Why our enthusiasm? It is not just that as taxpayers we welcome a drive for more efficiency in managing the public purse. It is because that is the only way to put the 'smaller but better' slogan of Options for Change into practice. Because of excessive bureaucracy, cumbersome structures and overmanned management machinery, too much money has been absorbed into what we might call overhead and the actual money spent on equipment has been squeezed accordingly.[2]*

This statement sits pretty comfortably with much of what I have said in the previous chapters, so it came as little surprise to me that industry viewed things this way. The Defence Costs Study was of course a great opportunity, and it is sad that as such it was wasted in terms of procurement. I will investigate that wasted opportunity in a later chapter.

Defence equipment procurement can perhaps be thought of as a three-legged stool, with the field user (represented by the Operational Requirements staff), the Procurement Executive and industry providing the three legs. The legs must each be of much the same strength, with the user dictating the requirement, accepting the finished article and using it in training and on operations; the Procurement Executive writing the technical specification and contract, and supervising development and production; and industry designing, developing and fabricating the equipment. Provided those three groups are involved properly throughout the procurement cycle, the three legs are of the same length and the procurement seat is level and stable. Even if one of the three legs is shortened a little, the seat, although tipped, will remain stable, as the system is flexible. Regrettably this stool with three legs of roughly equal strength and length is only an idealist's dream. In reality, the stool has four legs, the fourth being the central programming and financial scrutiny staff: excessively powerful but extremely short in involvement and knowledge. The Sir Humphrey Applebys will

> *give it the most serious and urgent consideration but will insist on a thorough and rigorous examination of all the proposals, allied to a detailed feasibility study and budget analysis, before producing a consultative document for consideration by all interested bodies and seeking comments and recommendations to be incorporated in a brief for a series of working parties who will produce individual studies that will form the background for a more wide-ranging document considering whether or not the proposal should be taken forward to the next stage.[3]*

Although this is quoted from a *Yes, Prime Minister* programme about the national education service, it has many of the hallmarks of procurement attitudes in the rarefied atmosphere of the sixth floor of the Main Building in Whitehall. The whole of the passage can be reduced to two words: 'Delay it.'

We have already looked at the inhabitants of the Main Building, and it is now time to examine the world of the 'tradesmen', as the members of the Procurement Executive and industry are sometimes slightingly described.

Dr Malcolm McIntosh, recently Chief of Defence Procurement, believed 'that the PE is a highly professional organisation'[4], whereas his director at the time, Air Commodore Martin Palmer, who has since retired from the RAF, saw 'increasing professionalism in the PE with better training and good quality staff'.[5] This suggests that it was not yet, in his opinion, highly professional. Other people are much less charitable. The Operational Requirements staff are repeatedly made aware of the very severe shortcomings of those they deal with in the Procurement Executive, and frustration at the shoddy and amateur way in which business is done is widespread.

At the head of this chapter I quote from the SIP Industry Consultation Study, a supreme example of wasted money which I shall look at later. It does, however, contain an interesting selection of views, mostly anonymous but nevertheless authentic. According to the report:

> *The expertise of Procurement Executive project managers was widely questioned by defence suppliers, in particular their lack of knowledge and experience in key technical areas ... there was perceived to be a serious lack of risk management skills and practices ... MOD is perceived to be a bureaucratic dinosaur ... mountains of documentation ... endless committees ... difficulties in establishing where the buck stops ... slow decision making ... it is believed that the Procurement Executive is not organised for effective management.*

Admittedly this was the view of industrialists and they would say that, wouldn't they? What about the views of those in the Procurement Executive? The report goes on to record the following internal views:

> MOD staff and especially those from the Procurement Executive were even harsher in their judgements on their own performance. People saw their organisation as too bureaucratic, unresponsive and inflexible to cope ... too many vested interests ... people and agencies bearing influence on progress without any responsibility ... the lack of any unifying shared vision or common values and goals.

and reports the views of 'the people at the coal face':

> A need for more authority, a need for more knowledge, a need for organisational support, a need to set up and develop more integrated, multi-disciplinary teams, a concern as to where the next generation of managers will come from.[6]

There is a lot more. I could name one directorate in the Procurement Executive where management is so bad that every single project I looked at within its area was slipping badly: sometimes the main fault lay with industry but little or no firm action had been taken by the MOD project managers or programme director; often all the fault lay within the Procurement Executive. Hardly what I would call a professional outfit, Dr McIntosh.

So why is the performance so lacking in professionalism? We have already examined the dead hand of high-level bureaucracy of the fat, squat leg of our four-legged stool, and of the military user. Let us now look at the two remaining legs, beginning with the Procurement Executive.

Rather than looking at each of the three main groups – Project Management, Contracts and Finance & Secretariat (F&S – yet more financial scrutineers!) – it is more interesting to examine their performance by looking at those aspects which repeatedly impact adversely on the long-suffering user: cost escalation, time delay and weak contracts.

My First Law of Procurement states:

All cost estimates are wrong.

Of course they are wrong, as it is decreed that the costs not only for development and production but also for spares, training and 20 to 30 years in-service running have to be estimated accurately before the staff target can be endorsed by EAC, Treasury and Minister prior to the feasibility study. Any revision after that is treated as a crime, bringing in its train yet more detailed scrutiny and agonising over whether the project should continue or not. Overestimate initially and you may get no funding at all or, if you do, other projects get unnecessarily dislodged from the overall equipment programme; underestimate and you are accused of 'cost growth' and 'entryism', and the financiers call for cancellation. Estimation of procurement costs can only be done reasonably accurately once project definition is complete, but even then whole life costs are still fairly vague. Nevertheless, costs for the first ten years are the most crucial and estimation later in the procurement cycle is the only answer to getting these costs more accurate.

But should the cost estimates be quite so inaccurate? We should be able to do better. Regrettably, however, the F&S staff are administrative civil servants rather than professional technical cost estimators and have no technical training. They have, and can have, no knowledge of what they are costing. There are of course some exceptions to this, but by and large the F&S staff are pretty clueless as to what should be costed and, worse, what they have costed. This is illustrated every year in the annual summer-long 'screening' process when every single project is scrutinised, supposedly in depth, but actually rather superficially. So often at these meetings the F&S expert is extraordinarily vague as to what is and what is not included. Even VAT gets left out when it should be in and included when it should be left out.

The project managers can help but often have no time to check detailed workings. Hardly surprising when it is not their job. Sometimes the user does it for them through sheer frustration. I walked into a 'screening' meeting late on one occasion to hear the Operational Requirements major talking. I got my papers out and settled in. He was still talking: about costs, and about how the costings were carried out. The F&S principal asked him questions about what they had done. The major told them. He knew because he had spent hours making sure that F&S got their costs correct. Like the child who gets his dad to do his homework for him and cannot explain his working to the teacher the next day, the F&S staff were clearly demonstrating similar ignorance of their workings.

In early 1995, a different major came to me with the committee submission for a certain project. I questioned him on the costings. He answered in detail. I asked him who had done them and it transpired that he had done them himself. Why did he do this, as it was not his job and he worked long enough hours (probably 15 hours per week longer than those whose work he was doing)? According to him he had been discussing the costs and had insisted that certain things had to be included. Too difficult, was the reply. In frustration, he did it himself. Was his work accurate? Possibly not, but surely more accurate than work which deliberately left several key costs out of account.

This is nothing new. I remember a senior Army man in the Procurement Executive lamenting that each costing he examined was like a blob of mercury – it dispersed into tiny pieces whenever he put his finger on it. But it seems to be getting worse. It appears the Procurement Executive now has little ability to understand costs submitted by industry. Reliance on competition to force down industrial costs seems to have eroded to a dangerous degree the ability to examine costs. Reliance on consultants is the favourite way out – but at a cost, and often without any improvement in understanding.

The second great failing is time delay. The belief in many parts of MOD is that projects take 30 per cent longer than estimated originally. This is nonsense: delays are much greater, although I have to admit the baseline is rarely clear-cut. Before talking to an Army Command and Staff Course, I did a little exercise. With no premeditated selection, I wrote down a dozen or so large projects which had recently entered, or were about to enter, service with the British Army. I then traced the anticipated in-service date (at which the equipment was expected to be first deployed with the Army) at the first committee submission, which was normally at the staff target stage immediately before the feasibility study. I compared this with the actual time taken. The result was surprising. Not so much the fact that these projects took twice as long as expected, but that in every case bar one the time overrun was almost exactly 100 per cent. This did not seem to be related to the technical or managerial complexity of the project. The hugely challenging Rapier Field Standard C development scored much the same in time delay as the AS 90 programme which was completed largely by private venture funding before MOD came on the scene. Both were 'good' projects. Others which were 'bad' projects, with weak management in MOD and in industry, seemed to fare no worse. Surprisingly, there appears to be no common denominator, yet the delay is largely constant.

So my Second Law of Procurement states that:

All major equipment projects take twice as long as envisaged originally.

Some of the causes can be laid at the door of MOD decision-making bureaucracy, about which I have said a great deal already. Others can be laid at industry's feet and we will come back to these later in this chapter. Most, however, must be pinned securely on extraordinarily poor project management at all levels from the members of the project teams upwards.

At the very top level, there is a lack of true knowledge of the state of individual projects. Project managers, programme directors and directors general are often unwilling to portray problems in stark detail. They paint over the problems and point up the achievements. I am sure they do not really believe that the bearer of bad news will be shot, but they behave as if they did. Everybody in fact behaves as if they were issued with rose-coloured glasses when joining the Procurement Executive. I know from my time in project management that no such glasses are issued; I also know that senior managers hate owning up to problems, slips, cost escalation and other bad news. Much easier to sweep it under the carpet, cross your fingers and hope it will all magically come right before the next exposure. Vain hopes! But the senior manager will have moved on by then.

Project managers and programme directors are generally very weak indeed. They lack the ability to look ahead beyond the immediate crisis, they often have little background in the areas of their responsibility, and they lack firmness when dealing with their superiors and with industry. Most project managers are from the scientific and technical civil service. They joined to carry out research, not to become managers, and so they have few of the right qualities. There are some good ones, but very few. Some of the best disappear: Steve Gibbs, for example, who was seconded to the Docklands Light Railway in its darkest hour, has not come back. Many of the military project managers are second-rate as well. Indeed, the worst are quite on a par with the worst of the technical civilians, but for different reasons: they generally have the right qualities but lack background and training in procurement, at least in the depth that would make sense. Amongst all this mediocre or poor quality, it is a pleasure to work with really good project managers. By far the best, in my experience, were two very dissimilar characters: Peter Merritt and Andrew Pinion.

Peter was an administrative civil servant and the only project manager I know to have come from such a background. He was talkative and friendly, but sharp as a freshly steeled carving knife. He was not a technician but he knew which technical advisers he could trust; he had an instinct for correct facts. He was clear-sighted, impossible to sidetrack from the main issues, tough, determined and a winner. He got results. His management of the very highly technical Rapier programme was exemplary: it would have swamped a lesser man. He was reported to have told a younger, less experienced colleague: 'There are rules and there are rules. The trick is to discover which rules you cannot break and then bend the others as far as you can.' Sadly, Peter is no longer with us; MOD is much the poorer for that.

Andrew, now retired, was the military project manager of the AS–90 self-propelled howitzer which was deployed in the British Army on the day he retired. Although technically an easier programme, there were many problems; in fact, the difference in project complexity tends to disappear in late development as the early high risk is eliminated. Andrew was in many ways the very antithesis, at least superficially, of the popular concept of a modern technical project manager: florid, moustached, rotund, he appeared at first sight to be a rather old-fashioned officer of the old brigade. Nothing was further from the truth, unless it was his encyclopaedic knowledge of artillery, a subject that is sadly out of fashion amongst many artillerymen today. He was tough, clear-headed and absolutely opposed to accepting less than full compliance. He was, however, extremely constructive in his opposition, always exploring sensible ways in which the problem could be overcome without damage to the overall outcome. A much respected man; an ideal man, in fact, to remain in project management, working his way upwards using his experience. But he was 55 and therefore officially too decrepit to serve any longer. He was shown the door marked 'Retirement'.

Both proved to be capable, self-confident men completely dedicated to an outstanding product. They were a pleasure to deal with. Not so other project managers, many of whom are weak professionally, inexperienced in the field in which they are currently working, lacking in pride in their product, and too keen to find the easy way out in the short term – usually a route which conflicts with the long-term interest. They stumble from crisis to crisis. Some areas are worse than others but the worst are bad indeed. Unsurprisingly, it is areas where civilian and military work side by side, each bringing his or her own strengths to the team, each learning skills and values from the other, that produce the best answers. Equally unsurprisingly, it appears that the policy is to completely civilianise the Procurement Executive. We all know the saying: 'If it ain't broke, don't fix it.' It seems that too often MOD takes the attitude: 'If it ain't broke, break it.'

My Fourth Law of Procurement simply states:

Contracts negotiated by MOD with industry always leave MOD in a weak legal position.

It is difficult to test the quality of a contract until problems arise. Problems arise throughout development and production, but they become acute towards the end of development and during the transition to production when time for solving them is fast running out. It is at this stage that the contract is really tested for the first time. Those under such test over the last few years were originally let in the mid- to late 1980s, and they are proving to be pretty disastrous. I would be a rich man if I had £100 for every time I have heard the pronouncement: 'Legal advice is that we do not have a strong position.'

I would hope that recent contracts have benefited from an understanding of these difficulties and will stand up better when tested at the end of this decade or the beginning of the next. I am not optimistic: we do not seem to be very good at learning from experience. Yet learning from the experience of others is vital if our contracts staff, spread thinly right across the Procurement Executive and attached to each project area, are to write strong contracts. None of them writes contracts for large projects on a regular basis; many are doing so, at working level, for the first time each time. They are thus inexperienced when the negotiations get going in earnest. Perhaps this would not matter too much if the contracts staff was of a high quality. But like the financial staff, they are administrative civil servants and not professional contract officers. They are also paid less than their industrial counterparts. Not surprisingly, they are less effective. We need high-quality professional contract writers and negotiators, and this means paying them properly. We do not, and so we get what we deserve.

Speaking at King's College London in 1994, the former Prime Minister John Major quoted Professor Michael Howard who, when discussing the military consequences of uncertainty and unpredictability in 1974, had said: 'I am tempted indeed to declare dogmatically that, whatever doctrine the armed forces are working on now, they have got it wrong'. Relax, Director Land Warfare, as you slave away at yet another step towards the new Army Doctrine which, some seven years after the fall of the Wall, is still in its infancy, for Howard went on to say:

I am also tempted to declare that it does not matter that they have got it wrong. What does matter is their capacity to get it right when the moment arrives.

Major developed this as follows:

For my part I am tempted to agree. But I would just observe that the speed with which significant forces can be brought to bear, and applied with precision has increased as a result of the development of greater strategic mobility, cruise missiles and so on. So the breathing space we have in which to adapt our forces through regrouping, retraining – or even sacking peacetime commanders! – is less than in the past.[7]

Yes, Prime Minister! He was undoubtedly right. For my part I am confident that we will regroup, retrain and even sack peacetime commanders if necessary – even in the shortened time now available. What I am not confident of is our ability to provide the right weapons and equipment in that reduced warning time if we have got it wrong. We did so in the Falklands and in the Gulf to a greater or lesser extent, but to do so successfully in the future presupposes three things: a competent Procurement Executive, a Defence Research Agency highly expert in all areas, and a substantial industrial base.

The decline of the defence budget has placed very great strain on the defence industry and many thousands of jobs have been lost. It is estimated that for every £1bn cut from the equipment programme, between 40,000 and 45,000 jobs are lost in the defence and supporting industries. This is grim enough for UK plc, but it gets worse. We have no government industrial strategy and MOD is tasked to look for a solution based solely on cost-effectiveness. With fair competition, this often means a foreign, government-supported winner. This further weakens the UK industrial base so that each time round any UK proposal will be weaker and a foreign winner more likely. It will not be long before British industry will be unable to compete in that particular area at all. But we are still not finished. MOD financial planning more and more favours buys 'off the shelf' (for obvious short-term financial reasons), which means production from whatever source without MOD subsidising development. For medium and large projects, industry cannot fully fund development, particularly when there is no guarantee that it will end up with a production order. Without development work, British industry will soon be reduced to a position in which all it can do is to pick up the crumbs of 'metal bashing' from US or European prime contractors. And what do the Service users get? Not what they require, not when they want it, and not what is value for money, except occasionally.

Whose side are we on? UK plc's or foreign industry's? The answer is obvious: in pursuing short-term 'value for money', we destroy our industrial capability in many areas and produce poor value for money in the long term.

I believe there might be a change in attitude in MOD; there is certainly at last an awareness of the problems. Regrettably, however, the documents that have been produced on this subject are not worth much: lots of words but little substance. This is a government-wide issue and until MOD, the Department of Trade and Industry and the Treasury come to an agreed policy, nothing much is likely to happen. Are we all Neros, fiddling while Rome burns?

It is of course difficult to gauge relative cost-effectiveness of different options in the long term as we cannot even cost the short term accurately. Fortunately we have at last grown out of the simplistic 'lowest bid wins' policy – several projects can bear witness to the folly of that. We do try now to evaluate the best bid all round in terms of value for money, but this is very difficult in many instances when much detail of development or production is not clear. Two examples will suffice.

The first concerned a bilateral collaborative project. A key element of the evaluation was the ability of each competing firm to carry out a vital process efficiently and effectively. The winner later switched its production process to a subcontractor without the relevant expertise, entirely undermining the basis of the competition and, more importantly, undermining the quality of the production units. Fortunately it was discovered early enough to force the contractor to change back again.

The second example also concerned a collaborative project. A particular highly advanced electronic component was only made by American and Japanese firms. The Japanese components were preferable but the United States pointed to the risks of relying on parts from outside NATO, although of course we do this all the time. The United States, not surprisingly, wanted to use their own firm and the Europeans were happy enough to go along with this after only token resistance. Imagine our surprise and perturbation when we discovered, just at the time when Marcos was being deposed and chaos erupted, that the US component was made in the Philippines.

These may appear minor issues. If they were isolated instances we could rest comfortably; but they are not. We may have learned some lessons – I mentioned 'lowest bid wins' – but these are often quickly forgotten. Meanwhile MOD procurement dogma is forever waiting in the wings, slavering at the mouth, ready to pounce on any idea with any juicy merit. Dogma is the real evil as it prohibits thought and forces all pegs, be they round, triangular, hexagonal or as yet merely undefined in shape, into square holes. No argument – do it.

Actually there is not just one dogma but many. Not just one dogma with several dangerous heads like Cerberus, guardian dog of the underworld, but many separate dogmas, like so many rottweilers awaiting the unwary. One of these rottweilers, by the name of international collaboration, recently slipped its leash and savaged a major project: the multi-role armoured vehicle (MRAV). As reported in *The Times* of 22 February 1995, the request to France and Germany for the United Kingdom to join their bilateral programme provoked deep alarm amongst chiefs of Britain's three armoured vehicle companies, who argued that MOD could get a more appropriate and cheaper vehicle through a domestic competition. Of course they would say that, wouldn't they? But in this case they would seem to be absolutely right. Who let this particular dogma off its leash is not clear, but undoubtedly it was someone in the Procurement Executive. Ignoring the views of the Operational Requirements staff, it was suddenly announced that the United Kingdom would apply to join a Franco–German collaborative programme which was far advanced but not clearly on the lines that the UK user required. Nevertheless, procurement staff flashed backwards and forwards between London, Paris and Bonn, discussing time scales, bar chart plans, deadlines and designs. They seemed curiously uninterested in discussing major procurement issues, such as competition (out of the question as far as the French were concerned), value for money, production methods, or, above all, the question of work shares for British industry. To a relative outsider, it seemed unlikely that with a French prototype already in existence and the French government standing firm against realistic competition, there would be anything substantial in it for British firms. If there had been major operational or financial advantage to be gained, sacrificing British industry might have been worthwhile to MOD, at least in the short term; but sacrificing British industry and probably longer-term competitive options for something that was not really what the user wanted and promised to give poor value for money seems absolutely ludicrous. It took much effort to put this particular rottweiler back into its kennel and nurse the victim back to health. The nursing was all but successfully completed when the dogma pounced again and finished the victim off. It is true that the MRAV project became the political entry fee to the new European Arms Agency, but this happened subsequently to the ill-judged procurement initiative. It has hardly given industry much confidence that a change of position is really on the agenda in MOD.

Another dogma which was let out a few years ago masqueraded as a poodle. What a wheeze to allow industry the honour of helping MOD finance development of major projects – wouldn't they just love the chance of putting their hands in their pockets to fund development 50:50? Perhaps they would. But did anyone think about the effect on competition, property rights or end product? Which bits would be funded by industry and which by MOD? Would industry be happy to pay up for development when the chance of a production order in a competitive programme was 50 per cent or less? Where would all this leave the losers, or the users? We have discovered that this poodle is yet another rottweiler. No terminal damage has yet been done but the writing is appearing on the wall: damage to MOD in that one hugely important programme has already slipped two years and more slip is likely; damage to the industrial losers will be clear in due course.

All in all, a sorry tale. The introduction of tough competition in the mid-1980s by Sir Peter Levene is not the issue; as Weston said:

We acknowledge that the MOD approach to competition policy in recent years has helped us in our own efforts to make ourselves more efficient.[8]

Despite the high cost of participating in the larger competitions (the attack helicopter competition is supposed to have cost each competitor between £50m and £100m just to produce a bid that could be taken seriously), competition has helped industry to become more efficient and, at the same time, it has saved MOD large sums of money. These savings have not been reinvested for the future, however, but have disappeared into the peace dividend or have been squandered by Whitehall inefficiency. Not content with that, we continue to inflict yet more difficulties on British industry: we lengthen procurement time scales by more and more convoluted decision-making; we reduce production volume more than necessary by breaking it into 'tranches' and putting later tranches out to competition; we impose 'off-the-shelf' dogma whether it is suitable or not to MOD, let alone industry; we become more and more risk-aversive and pin it all on the prime contractor; we give industry the slenderest encouragement and the minimum guarantee. And when we have done all this we turn our back and collaborate with other nations which have strong industrial policies, including financial support, without any thought of fighting properly for British industry's position. In 1994, a report by Ernst and Young, quoted in the *US Defense News*, criticised the extent to which MOD adheres to free-market policies, thereby making British industry vulnerable to international competition. The report went on to say that foreign industry often has the benefit of considerably greater government support in research and development funding, the French, for example, spending 60 per cent more than the United Kingdom. It concluded that our defence industrial base will be eroded to the point where it is no longer competitive internationally unless the government takes corrective action.[9]

The government's support for British industry is still pitiful. The August 1995 clash between Michael Portillo, then Chief Secretary to the Treasury, and Michael Heseltine, then President of the Board of Trade, made public the demands of the Treasury hawks for yet more reductions in the government's financial support of industry which was already the lowest in the European Union. In any case, the part that goes to the defence sector is probably less than the £350m annual savings made through larger production runs for overseas sales and the £75m which are generated through levies. And then we say: 'Why don't you put in £100m to develop this project – who knows, you might win a production order if you're very lucky!' What would be your view if you were a shareholder?

Having said all this, I must point out that, although the British defence industry has become much more efficient, there is still a long way to go. In a presentation to the Defence Manufacturers Association in 1994, I listed what I thought was wrong with both MOD and industry:

MOD	**Industry**
Ponderous	Myopic higher management
Bureaucratic	Decision-shy middle managers
Slow	Lack of management expertise
Inflexible	No forward strategy
Risk-aversive	Bad news aversive
Overmanned	Corner-cutting to disaster
Too many management layers	
Lack of expertise	
No forward strategy	

It was striking that while my criticism of MOD was strongly resented by MOD members of the audience, my criticism of industry was roundly applauded by the industrial members. This makes an eloquent point about the inbuilt inertia in MOD

and its inability (or more probably its reluctance) to see its own problems. In contrast, industry has been changing fast for years and is able to recognise that there is still some way to go.

Whether it realises quite how far it still has to travel is less clear. Higher management is in thrall to the shareholders and so the future is bound by the next annual report. True forward planning is therefore not possible. Middle management, if competent, is unwilling or unable to persuade the bosses of the long-term arguments; if less than competent, it can be very weak indeed. I have seen some project managers I would not employ under any circumstances – weak, indecisive, unable to see the wider picture, only able to deal with one problem at a time and to see one step ahead. There is little use of management aids and little higher-level critical path analysis. As a consequence, the implications of any setback are not immediately clear, and it is therefore not surprising, with time scales being so critical, that decisions are made without the full facts – decisions that are later seen to be wrong.

Another favourite pastime is the cutting of corners to save time and money. Perhaps under trial a missile behaves wrongly. The right answer would be to find out what is wrong and fix it. A quicker way is to change a number of parameters and try again. If it then works, well and good, but you do not know what put it right and this may come back to haunt you in the future. If it still does not work, you do not know whether it is the old problem uncorrected or a new one created. These short-cuts, which are adopted often and enthusiastically, almost always end in disaster, in further delay and in further costs.

It is fashionable for industry to talk about partnerships with MOD, quoting relationships that they may create with certain trusted subcontractors. A very seductive idea, but what it actually means is less than clear. Any such 'partnership' must rely on trust on both sides. At present such trust does not exist. Industry cannot trust MOD when it sees its amateur management and its dogma in action, supporting the industry of other nations at least as well, if not more, than its own. MOD cannot trust industry for realistic costs and competent management. Until these short-comings are tackled realistically, mutual trust is unlikely to flower.

There is precious little evidence that, on the MOD side, the shortcomings are recognised at all. The almost paranoid reactions to my criticisms smack of laager mentality, as the wagons are formed into a defensive circle to repel the ignorant savages on the outside who wish to change certain aspects of the defenders' central tenets of faith. Maybe there is some doubt in the higher echelons of MOD – not about MOD competence or central dogma, but about fine-tuning it and gaining even better value for money. If there is doubt, can reorganisation be far behind? In fact the Procurement Executive has recently been reorganised; not to align itself with organisations elsewhere in MOD, such as Operational Requirements or the Defence Research Agency, but in an egocentric effort to improve its own internal management. The result is that those in the Operational Requirements staff and in the logistic organisations have to deal with more and more project managers and programme directors in the Procurement Executive. This can hardly be called efficient.

But then, just as the new organisation is attempting to settle down, the whole Procurement Executive is moved out of London to a faraway site at Abbey Wood, near Bristol. These two events will reduce output seriously. Although the official line has been that there will be no drop in output, there is no-one who believes this – indeed, most are convinced that there will be a vast reduction in effectiveness. This has already begun, leading primarily to delays in signing contracts, assessing competition, writing committee submissions and making costings. Most put this drop at around 20 or 30 per cent for a year, but some suggest it is likely to be more like 50 per cent for two years. Yet no forward plans appear to have been made to buy in extra staff, to reduce bureaucracy or to streamline procedures. Inevitably, projects will be held up, more strain will be put upon users and industry, and the huge resulting underspend will return not to the Defence Budget but to the Treasury.

Not only has the Procurement Executive been made to reorganise and move concurrently, but also to cope with a new IT system at Abbey Wood. A senior industrialist was amazed. In industry, he said, each of these three activities was viewed as a major disruption; to do all three at the same time was crazy. We must all hope for a miracle.

The short-term effect is one thing; the long-term implications are even more serious. Until now, staff in the Procurement Executive have worked extremely closely, if not always harmoniously, with the Operational Requirements staff and other key branches in the Central Staffs, OMB and single-Service staffs. Personal contact has been frequent, often several times a day, and this has only been feasible because offices were at most 20 minutes apart. It has been possible to have a 15-minute head-to-head confrontation (or should I say robust discussion?) to sort out a particular problem and to be back in the office in less than an hour. This is not possible now that Abbey Wood is occupied. However much travelling is undertaken, these short, informal get-togethers are a thing of the past, with the potential for considerable loss of understanding on each side. Instead of a typical marriage in which argument, understanding and give-and-take are merged into a working relationship, there will be a separation which is bound to end in divorce.

It is astounding that there has been little or no high-level consideration of the implications of the move to Abbey Wood and of how the staff will work with those remaining in London. It was suggested at one point that the Operational Requirements staff move to Abbey Wood as well. This is of course impractical as their links with the Programmes and Plans staffs, with the Central Scientific staffs and with the OMB (all of which are remaining in London) are fragile and would break if stretched 70 miles to Abbey Wood rather than the 70 metres or so which is the current stretch in the Main Building. The link between Operational Requirements and the Procurement Executive is much more robust and will be made to work at long distance. But this link will inevitably be more tenuous. There is a distinct danger that Abbey Wood will become an ivory tower. If this happens, what price a clutch of Nimrods?

In summary, MOD equipment procurement is amateur in most areas. The Defence Costs Study was a great opportunity to improve matters but it was, as far as equipment procurement is concerned, an opportunity missed. Reorganisation and the move of the Procurement Executive to Abbey Wood is going to make matters worse. This is bad news, not only for the equipment user, the soldier in the field, but also for the British defence industry. In other words, it is bad for UK plc. It is in the national interest to make MOD equipment procurement more efficient with less expensive overheads. We appear to be going in the opposite direction.

CHAPTER EIGHT

The Disaster That Is
Information Technology

*Congressional investigators said Tuesday that the Government wasted
billions of dollars a year on computers and that the machines were
often obsolete by the time they were installed.*
NEW YORK TIMES, FAX DIGEST, 12 OCTOBER 1994

*Long term improvements in Software Intensive Project procurement will
require more than skindeep changes to processes or procedures.*
MOD SIP CONSULTATION STUDY, 1994

In December 1994, the TV programme *World in Action* looked at waste of money
by government or public bodies. A significant part of the programme, and the
dominant part in terms of the size of waste, was devoted to computers. It described
a £2.6bn computer system which was a complete failure and a £48m system which
no-one wanted; it claimed that several hundred tons of computer equipment were
dumped on the scrap heap every year; that in the last 12 years £5bn had been
wasted; that consultants cost £500m per year and yet were under no control and
sometimes had no idea what the overall system was expected to do. In general it put
its finger on the main cause: no-one really thought through what was required.

While the media often sensationalise, distort and magnify the real issues out of
all proportion, the 'facts' reported in that programme ring pretty true, if only
because of the large number of Information Technology (IT) disasters that are
known to have occurred – not only in the United Kingdom, as the quote at the head
of this chapter shows. There are, of course, several reasons for problems in procurement, particularly where the project is technically complex. All major IT
projects are certainly that, but are they any more complex than, for example, a
nuclear submarine or a cruise missile? The problems may be different but the level
of complexity is just as high. Indeed you could justifiably claim that as IT is a major
part of such weapon systems, indeed almost any major weapon, an IT system on its
own has to be much less complex. It is not, therefore, the technical complexity
which is the root cause.

IT specialists are quick to claim that the speed of development in the IT world creates special problems and that procurement must be quick and the buy thrown away after very few years of Service: what I call the IT-profligate society. As considerable amounts of software are embedded in all modern weapons and platforms, this hardly makes a special case for IT-only systems. While the IT specialists are correct in criticising MOD procurement of software-intensive projects and in calling for more than skin-deep changes, they are wrong in asking for special procedures for such projects. All projects need major changes in procurement procedures. It would be yet another missed opportunity if IT specialists were to obtain changes in procedures just for major software-intensive projects.

These major changes must speed up the procurement cycle and ensure that improvements to the system can be made easily and relatively cheaply at the necessary points in the lifecycle; 'technology insertion', as the jargon has it. There is nothing here that is specific to IT. This must be done without jettisoning sensible checks and balances during development or reducing the useful life of the system significantly. In other words, risks and whole-life costs must be clearly established and accepted.

This appears to be anathema to the MOD IT world. They claim that it is not possible, that system life is very short, that MOD cannot influence the IT industry as it is only a small and usually special customer. It may be true that the IT industry will take little or no heed of MOD requirements, but in fact these requirements are little different from those of the IT world at large. The IT industry is not serving the interests of its customers but imposing its own terms on them; the real tragedy is that the customers accept this without understanding what is actually happening. The root cause of the repeated disasters in today's IT world of procurement is a lack of customer understanding.

Of course there are clever people who understand IT and who are paid large sums of money to spend huge amounts of a company's assets on new or upgraded IT systems. They are not, however, subject to the same knowledgeable or reasonably informed supervision and control as other spending departments. I suspect there is a million times more expertise at board level of a major company on new manufacturing facilities for mechanical components than there is on IT control systems. This should not matter because the control should come through a clear view of what is required, not on how it is to be designed. All too often this clear view of what IT systems have to do appears to be non-existent, as the *World in Action* programme highlighted. IT enthusiasts speak a language of their own which develops more rapidly than a non-expert can cope with, and they are happy talking this language which no-one else really understands (many claim they do of course!) and designing systems without bothering with a defined requirement. Why are they allowed to get away with it? Would you hire a builder to extend your house and allow him to talk about materials and techniques in a jargon you cannot understand without having given him clear instructions about the use and overall size, shape and position of the extension? Of course not. If you did, you could hardly be surprised if you ended up with an extension that is too big or too small, of a shape and position which precludes its use for what you had in mind, and with materials you dislike. Yet high-level managers express surprise when they take delivery of a less than useful IT system. They are baffled because they have paid millions of pounds to consultants to get it right, but fail to realise that they have omitted to lay down the exact requirement in advance.

The picture is the same in MOD. High-level managers have little knowledge, even less interest and no confidence at all in their ability to think through the requirement. Their reaction has been to throw money and specialists at a problem they do not comprehend. The specialists spend the money, talk gibberish and end up with too many unsatisfactory projects, both operational and non-operational. The facts can be summed up in two sentences:

- The British Army has no operational all-arms command and control IT system of any sort in Service now.
- The MOD Operational Requirements staff have had imposed on it a user-unfriendly office IT system (CHOTS) which cannot interface with the IT systems of the majority of other MOD departments with which it does business.

Let us look at these two statements in a little more detail. The Army has recently taken delivery of two IT systems, BATES and ADCIS. BATES is a command and control system for the tasking and co-ordination of indirect fire artillery, and the lowest level is already deployed in the field. ADCIS is its counterpart in the world of Army air defence and has gone through its user trials successfully to ensure that it meets the requirement. Both BATES and ADCIS have been developed to meet detailed and clear operational requirements. Both, so far as they have been trialled, meet requirements, are within cost and are welcomed by the user in the field. There have been delays but these are consistent with the sizes of delay experienced across the board as mentioned in an earlier chapter. Success? Yes, but not according to the IT specialists. They maintain that both systems are old-fashioned and could be much better. So they could – but they work. The IT specialists also claim that today's soldiers, who are experienced with modern computer displays, will not take seriously displays which look decidedly old-hat. During the trials, I specifically questioned soldiers using ADCIS for the first time about the displays. All were enthusiastic. Many commented on how easy they were to use; others said that their eyes did not get as tired with prolonged use as with many more modern displays. Everybody said how easy the training was, even those who had never operated a computer of any sort before.

The real motive behind this IT opposition is that BATES and ADCIS are the only operational systems in Service with the Army, but neither was developed under the eye of the MOD's IT specialists. The requirements were written by non-IT specialists in the Royal Artillery who, together with the Procurement Executive, oversaw development. The IT specialists were away with the birds writing 'overarching strategies', 'vision statements', interface specifications, standards and so on, none of which seems to have produced much overall output. A touch of 'not invented here' as befits anyone who is or pretends to be a bit of a scientist!

Meanwhile, the all-arms commanders at all levels from corps down to company level, or even below, have no IT system at all to help with their decision-making, battle appreciation or processing of orders, with the exception of a few computers bought in a hurry for the Gulf War and since upgraded. In fact, little or no progress has been made in this area at all that is visible to the soldier in the field. Progress has been held up while the IT specialists have been preparing their battlefield IT strategy. Four years and several forests have been consumed in the process, but the light at the end of the tunnel hardly equates to a torch beam looking for the enemy at 400 metres range. Fortunately the 'strategy' is 'complete', so the real work has begun. With the bureaucratic procedures in the procurement chain, no resilient fieldable system is likely to be ready for a decade or so. Before this, I suspect, the 'strategy' will have been 'revised', leading to yet more delay.

The Army's battlefield IT strategy has been delayed and reduced to absurdity in any case by the inability of the Army to decide on what it wants. Hiding behind the notion that every commander exercises command in a unique way and that therefore stating the requirement is impossible, they have called for the 'whole world'. We want to know about the enemy, they say. What exactly do you want to know? Everything! *Everything* about *every* enemy logistic vehicle? Well, perhaps not, but everything else! Every hospital and ambulance? Stop being silly! We also want to know *everything* about our own forces. Everything? Everything! Does the corps commander want to know everything about every air defence resupply vehicle? You are just being difficult, you know what I mean. As an IT specialist I don't, but I'll go away and do it my way! I'll deliver you the 'whole world', at a price, within a reasonable time scale if you don't interfere. Another recipe for disaster.

The Army has not been very clever operationally, although the position is now acknowledged and much energy is being expended in closing the gap in a hurry. On the non-operational front MOD has not been any cleverer. In an interview with *Preview* in 1994, Air Commodore Martin Palmer, then Director of Procurement Policy (Studies), said:

> *Collocation [of the Procurement Executive at Abbey Wood] will, I think, be a good thing, but the Department will still have to guard against its tendency to think in sectors. The Procurement Executive is not an entity in itself, it is part of the process and it must never lose sight of that. The interface with the Operational*

Requirements staff and Principal Administrative Officers [QMG for the Army]
is equally important and will have to be managed. Careful thought is needed about
the electronic interfaces and how we manage data.[1]

Sadly this is all too late. No thought appears to have been given to electronic
interfaces within MOD as a whole, with the result that within the equipment procurement world, the four main groups (Operational Requirements, Procurement
Executive, Defence Research Agency and the Field Army) have no electronic links
with each other at all. Nor will they have in the foreseeable future. Desk officers in
Operational Requirements can e-mail others in the same building, but they do not
need to make use of this very often – if the facility was not available they could easily telephone or walk the short distance. However, most of their business is done
away from their own building with directorates and agencies spread right across the
United Kingdom with whom they have no common electronic interface at all.
Instead the desk officers are saddled with the remarkably unpopular CHOTS system, which many believe to be not worth upgrading and in need of scrapping in a
few years' time. Not very surprisingly, both the Procurement Executive and the
Defence Research Agency have gone for something else – but not the same something else.

On viewing a prototype of the Procurement Executive's future IT system
DAWN, the Chief of Defence Procurement said: 'It is absolutely vital that we get
our IT right.'[2] How right he was! Yet DAWN caters only for the Procurement
Executive internally, not for the vital external links to MOD in Whitehall and elsewhere. Rightly the CDP does not want CHOTS, but he will have to accept a small
number of CHOTS terminals just to provide the electronic link from Abbey Wood
to the Main Building. Has he pressed the Operational Requirements world in
London to accept DAWN instead of CHOTS? I doubt it. Yet DAWN would be of
more use to the Operational Requirements desk officer than is CHOTS. Has the
Operational Requirements hierarchy ever thought this through? No – for the simple reason that those with the responsibility for doing so only communicate with
others in the Main Building in Whitehall and do not appear to understand that there
is a problem.

DAWN will eventually, I understand, interface electronically with the defence
industry as a whole. Excellent – another very potent reason why Operational
Requirements should have DAWN. If it could then interface with, or be adopted by,
the Defence Research Agency, many of the day-to-day operating problems would
be eased. Regrettably, those that make these high-level decisions appear to be set on
keeping the Operational Requirements staff away from the benefits of the 1990s
electronic office. Keep that forked stick in good repair, lads, and increase your travel
budget!

Just as the Army has failed to think through the exact requirement for an all-arms IT system, and just as various non-defence bodies have failed to think through exactly what they want their IT system to do, so those in charge of CHOTS have failed, too. In June 1994, when CHOTS had 'a substantial body of users', Dr Michael Harte, Director General of Information Technology Systems (DGITS) and the man responsible for delivering CHOTS, said:

> *The organisation is having to think very hard about how it is going to use CHOTS for daily business. We may be good at handling data but we have not got very far in information management. What does PUS [the MOD Permanent Under Secretary] need to know to run his organisation? Indeed what do I, as DGITS, need to know to run mine? It's not a concept that we have thought about very much.*[3]

If this is so, it would be surprising, were the failure to think through the requirement not so common in the whole IT world. Can you imagine persuading MOD committees to place a production contract for armoured vehicles worth billions of pounds with industry with the major parameters undefined? The IT approach is a licence for IT specialists to waste the taxpayers' money while being paid handsomely. Sadly, this is a feature of the whole IT world, and not specific to MOD.

The fact is that IT specialists are allowed to live in their ivory tower, inventing their own language which frightens away outsiders and conferring an aura of omniscient wisdom on often mediocre people. This has many similarities with the Intelligence world, which is adept at sidestepping questions with a softly-breathed 'need to know' whether or not they know the answer. When I joined Technical Intelligence years ago, my predecessor made much of this technique to appear omniscient. I was responsible for 'non-communications electronics', a term unmatched for instant audience switch-off. My Intelligence boss told me in no uncertain terms that electronic terminology was a foreign language to most and that I was to use ordinary English in conversing with those with no electronic expertise. 'It can be done', he said. I did as I was told, and it was indeed possible. How can we persuade the IT world to use English rather than gobbledegook? With difficulty, because it requires thought. But it is essential as too many people, admittedly including myself, assume they know what the various terms mean when they don't and confusion ensues. We have a language which is fast becoming an international standard. Let us use it. It is called English.

We must not, however, go too far in the opposite direction and use over-simplistic language which carries no meaning. One example is the 1994 Study on Software-Intensive Projects carried out for the Procurement Executive and quoted at the beginning of this chapter. It set out to use clear English but only succeeded in becoming a laughing stock. Such examples as the following are surely meaningless, or worse, give the impression of talking down to the reader:

*It is not a yellow-brick road. It enables the magnitude of necessary improvements
to happen.*
*It is a syndrome. The relationship between 'doing' and 'being'. 'Doing' is the
reflection of 'being'.*
Communications provide the vehicle for conveying the information required.
Scaling Everest. Leave the peak alone.
We listened with the wings of our ears.[4]

Clearly, the answer is for the IT specialists to use English and not to employ non-specialists from outside to use it for them.

We must get the IT specialists out of their ivory tower and into the real world.
One reason why BATES and ADCIS have reached deployment to the British Army
is that their requirements were written by those who knew intimately the environment in which they were to work. The design was system requirement-oriented, not
IT-oriented. The systems were designed to serve the needs of guns and missiles, not
to serve the glory of IT. It is important that the future operational IT system, to
operate within armoured and infantry battlegroups and combat teams, is equally
requirement-oriented; it must be designed as an integral part of tanks and other
armoured vehicles or it will fail to deliver the necessary electronic support. It must
not be stolen from the Army by the IT specialists.

Reality is all important. One major issue demonstrates quite clearly the divorce
of the IT specialists from the real world: the issue of 'commercial off-the-shelf'
equipment or COTS (not to be confused with the MOD headquarters IT system,
CHOTS). For years the IT specialists have pursued a strategy to include as much
commercial equipment as possible that can be bought in the civilian market place
off the shelf. They claim that we cannot afford 'bespoke' hardware or software either
in financial or in time-scale terms. It is true that both initial procurement costs and
development time scales of COTS-based systems are a fraction of 'bespoke systems'. But with COTS-based systems there are also sizeable disadvantages. These
include security, property rights, risk acceptance and lack of control over replacement cycles. Industrial decisions, not military or MOD financial considerations,
determine replacement time scales, and this places a serious question mark over the
cost of ownership over, say, 30 years – in other equipment areas this would be called
'whole-life costs'. I have never managed to get the IT specialists to attempt a 30-year costing; all I get in lieu is a cracked 78 rpm record playing, 'We cannot afford
non-COTS equipment.' It is a bit like arguing with an answerphone.

There are, however, much more serious disadvantages with COTS, and these are
vulnerability to electronic battlefield attack, either nuclear or non-nuclear, and
insufficient general ability to withstand battlefield conditions in all parts of the
world. It seems fundamental to me that just as we insist that a tank survives in a
battlefield environment, we should also design battlefield IT systems to work in

those conditions. COTS-based systems are obviously more vulnerable than bespoke systems and this must be a major consideration. This is MOD policy, updated recently, and yet it is being flouted by the IT world. We must insist on the right level of electronic protection and ruggedness for our battlefield equipment. Once this is agreed, and the cost/time implications examined, the selection of COTS can be made with objective clarity. I have been labelled anti-COTS, which is not true. I am for the necessary quality of battlefield equipment; whether this includes or excludes COTS I am not worried. We must resist the COTS argument that runs something like this:

> *We cannot afford 'bespoke' systems, so we must make maximum use of COTS. COTS is vulnerable to battlefield conditions, so we must jettison defence standards, or indeed any standards on hardening against electronic attack, or resistance against nuclear, biological or chemical attack, or rugged performance in battlefield conditions. And no, I do not know the 30-year saving.*

Let us design for the battlefield, not the IT specialist or the accountant. The use of COTS then becomes a secondary issue. Can we tame the IT world and bend it to our real use? I doubt it, as I see little interest in high places in the fact that there is a disaster in progress. Pass the telescope and I'll put it to my blind eye.

CHAPTER NINE

International Jamborees

I travel not to go anywhere but to go. I travel for travel's sake.
ROBERT LOUIS STEVENSON, 'TRAVELS WITH A DONKEY'

It's alright for some', they always say when a busy executive returns from yet another trip abroad to the envious office-bound London staff, 'but someone has got to stay and do the work!' If they claim to be joking, it is only partly true. Most claim that they are not joking, envisaging sun-drenched days by the pool, exotic drinks, expensive meals, interesting sights, amusing companions with whom to do a little business.

The busy executive's view is different. A Sunday flight to the United States, followed by one or two internal flights to arrive at the hotel, hopefully pre-booked without a hitch, at around 4 a.m. British time, or 11p.m. local time. Jet lag sets in, making sleeping difficult. Up at 7 a.m. for breakfast and the drive to the huge complex where the meeting is to be held starting at 8 a.m. Windowless, with canned air and functional furniture, the conference room is only reached after successfully overcoming the vagaries of the security clearance system against which there is no appeal, and a quick return home waits for those who get it wrong or suffer a mistake in the system. A 15-minute coffee break, possibly with tempting doughnuts to undermine the waistline, lunch in a canteen at 11.30 a.m., the long slog through the afternoon and often early evening, until the return to your hotel in time for another assault on your waistline (there is, after all, nothing else to do in many American towns except eat, but there is plenty of opportunity to do that at low cost) and bed, to sleep or not as the jet lag takes you. Three more days of this sheer excitement and then it' s up early on Friday for the internal connections to make the London flight from Washington, New York, Dallas or Atlanta. Sleep if you can, but most arrive early on Saturday morning, feeling terrible and looking worse, without any feeling of having had a good time - except perhaps in terms of business done.

The truth lies somewhere in between. While many international meetings are of the type described above, some are spread conveniently over a weekend or run to a less intense schedule for various reasons. In Europe, unlike in the United States, meetings are usually held in major cities such as London, Paris, Rome and now Berlin, with countless attractions in the evenings, and, for those who get an hour or two off, by day as well. Some of these attractions may be within a few minutes' walk of the conference room or hotel.

At a higher level, there is more official entertainment. The Italians are by far the best at this. The biggest meal I have ever had was an official dinner in the Italian Parachute Regiment officers mess in Siena, and the most sumptuous setting of any official dinner I have been to was an old palazzo in Rome. The more senior the heads of delegation, the more extensive the social programme – not always at the expense of work, rather at the expense of sleep. Drafting statements or agreements at midnight after four hours of food and entertainment is not much fun; the alternative of an early call at 5 a.m. to do the same is only for the strong-minded.

Just how necessary is all this jetting back and forth? The simple answer is that if we are to collaborate internationally to produce common military equipment with longer production runs at lower cost, international meetings are a must. There is no substitute for the individuals in a working group getting together round a table or in a factory to discuss and decide. This must happen on a frequent basis if the project is not to be delayed or to get too far down a wrong alley. At a higher level, high frequency of meetings is not necessary but the senior managers still need to meet to thrash out matters of policy which cannot be decided lower down. For every project there must be many meetings at various levels throughout each year; with extensive international collaboration, there needs to be bi-, tri-, or multilateral meetings to discuss policy for future collaboration. The more we collaborate, the more international meetings that have to be attended.

International equipment collaboration has become a central policy plank for the United Kingdom, for Western Europe and to some extent for the United States. The major goal is common equipment with which an alliance can go to war, simplifying logistics, training and usage. Commonality and compatibility have long been established within the artillery worlds of the United Kingdom and the United States and more recently of France and Germany. This paid enormous dividends during the Gulf War when all the tube and rocket ammunition we needed to fire was available either from our own stocks or those of the United States. Commonality and compatibility in other areas is less widespread and in some non-existent. It is worth pursuing.

The most critical area of all is communications, yet here the goal of international compatibility is as far off as it is in any other area and, worse, appears to be receding. The difficulties of sharing extremely sensitive data on electronic protection measures and other aspects of electronic warfare, and the need to manufacture nationally have so far undermined all efforts, but is it not ridiculous to pretend to collaborate, yet ignore the one vital area? Another example of form instead of substance.

There is one major stumbling block which is far more difficult to overcome than sensitivity over detailed performance data or national production, and this is the obstacle of harmonising the various nations' needs, not so much in military requirement terms, although this problem should not be minimised, but in terms of time scale. The need to retain equipment in Service for as long as possible, with minimum spending on maintenance and enhancement, dictates equipment lives of 20 to 30 years. The chances of two countries sharing a common time scale for replacement is slim, dropping to nearly non-existent when the nations involved increase in number. There is only a certain leeway that can be achieved by pushing or pulling the replacement date; bring it forward significantly and the financiers, audit office and Parliament will smell a sharp reduction in value for money, even if money for an earlier replacement can be brought forward in the budget; push it back and running costs will threaten to escalate wildly.

Once a common time scale is agreed, common requirements ought to be plain sailing. But often this is not the case. There are some major differences in the way nations see a capability, often for historical reasons (the balance between a tank's protection, firepower and mobility is an example); but more often difficulties arise from a 'little Englander' mentality or 'de Gaulle chauvinism' rather than from a real difference of need. Once this obstacle has been overcome we run into the barrier of national industrial work shares. Each nation wants at least its fair share of high-technology work, rather than tin-bashing which is not much more than a sizeable lump of ballast. Carving up the high-tech work is difficult and often leads to inefficiencies, with parts of the equipment shuffled repeatedly to and fro between the various nations. There is much inefficiency in international collaboration, imposed by the nations for very good reasons. If we are becoming more flexible in our view of work share in the United Kingdom, this is not necessarily being followed in all other countries.

So far I have not mentioned NATO, despite the fact that the NATO Army Armaments Group and its naval and air force equivalents spend enormous effort in terms of conference time to establish common NATO projects. Despite all this effort, the track record of successful projects is woeful. The reason is simple: too many nations without the ability to find necessary funding spend much time objecting, changing, wrangling and insisting on requirement details, only to withdraw when the financial going gets tough. Many of the small nations have no real ability, or indeed need, to look more than five years ahead, and this sits most uncomfortably with the 20-year span of international collaborative programmes.

I well remember my first ever meeting at NATO Headquarters in Brussels in 1981. The major item on the agenda was the outline NATO staff target for an Army air defence system, the first tentative step on the path to a joint project. We were to discuss the aim of the document; the next part would be discussed at the following meeting six months later. With two meetings a year, it looked unlikely that the staff target would be ready before the mid-1980s, with a possible in-Service date some time at the beginning of the next century. I pointed this out and asked if anyone seriously believed the declared in-Service date for this project of – not 2000, or 1995, or even 1990, but 1985. In my view we would be lucky if the early stages of development would have started by then. The chairman had a fit. I was made to feel I was not being 'helpful'. Since then, the project has laboured on and is about to enter the early stages of development (project definition) for an in-Service date of 2015 or even later.

NATO projects are largely a waste of time but do act as some justification for the very large numbers of people on the international staff in Brussels. Successful international projects are usually the result of bi-, tri-, or quadrilateral discussions. Smaller nations often join in at a much later stage. I am sure there must be a mathematical relation between the increasing difficulties and delays in a project and the number of nations involved – exponential perhaps?

If there are no successful NATO projects, there are many successful international programmes. Few of these are major front-line weapon systems, particularly if you discount those that started as a national development in one country. I have described the successful MLRS terminally guided warhead munition, but of course this was cancelled just as it was about to prove the prototype in a full 'end-to-end' test. This sadly has to count as a project failure. SP70, the self-propelled howitzer for the 1970s (a bit of a misnomer as it would never have been deployed until the 1980s or, more likely, the 1990s) was another failure for a different reason: a fatal decision at the start – the German insistence on a rear-engine tank chassis led to challenges in automatic loading which proved impossible to overcome reliably – eventually put paid to this project. At the moment we have no common tank or armoured reconnaissance vehicle, no common small arms system, no common infantry carrier, no common army air defence weapon (although there just might be in 2020 or so), no common aircraft identification system, no common logistic vehicles, no common dry bridge, no common mine, no common command and control, no common communications system and no common helicopter. Are the other Services any better? Can the Tornado be called a success when it has to be replaced early? Will the Eurofighter be affordable? And where is the common frigate? The basic MLRS launcher and bomblet munition and the FH70 howitzer are about the only exceptions I can think of.

This is a bleak catalogue, but it is not quite so bad when we look at smaller projects with fewer virility overtones. The Anglo-German M3 ferry, the Anglo-German-French Cobra advanced weapon locating radar (which could still fail on price) and the medium-range Trigat anti-tank missile system spring readily to mind, but there are still not many of them. We have bought one another's finished equipment more plentifully and that seems to work well. The difficulty here is that, at least for large complex systems, it is a risky decision to buy a foreign ready-made solution in ten to fifteen years rather than to develop our own or collaborate with others on the development. Risky because we either have to accept an equipment that has been in Service with a foreign army for years and is obsolescent, or we make the decision on a paper system which does not yet exist and which can be cancelled or changed substantially for foreign national reasons without our input. We can hardly demand a say if we are not prepared to pay a share of development. There is another weakness: British industry gets no development and this weakens or even destroys its future ability to compete in that area. It is therefore hardly a policy option except at the lowest level where one national specialisation can be swapped for another without adverse effect on national industries or long-term planning.

The main options therefore remain national development or collaborative development, at least for the major weapons systems. And if collaborative development, which is claimed to be cheaper (mainly because of larger production runs), is to be a major activity, it follows that international meetings are a priority. So there will be a continued chorus of: 'It's alright for some'.

Although small in comparison with the supposed savings in collaborative development and production, the cost of all this travel is still large and needs to be minimised. There are three main activities concerning collaboration that result in frequent travel.

First, there are the committees and working groups directly associated with an international collaborative project. Although these need to be monitored continuously to ensure that each remains essential and cost-effective, it makes no sense to reduce the frequency of, or the attendance at, these groups below the essential. It could cost us out of all proportion.

Second, there are the high-level 'policy' fora at which senior people, from ministers down to about 1-star (brigadier or director level), meet their opposite numbers from other countries to discuss collaborative policy and future opportunities for collaboration, and to resolve knotty problems which have arisen from lower groups in NATO or multilateral project groups. These meetings are numerous and proliferating. They are pleasant, undemanding and usually of little direct benefit. There is much duplication. These meetings cannot all be ditched but some must be low priority. Some could be tagged onto the back of NATO meetings.

The third group is the most abused of them all: the grand tours, particularly to the United States, to 'see what's out there'. Many of these visits are ill-defined, lax in execution and duplicate the visits of others. They are not controlled, except by the British Embassy in Washington which is keen for many top-level officials and officers to visit. The squeeze gets put on the lower levels which I would argue are the most important. The trouble with central control is that no-one is in a good position to do it effectively; leave it to individuals and it is abused. It must be controlled within each area by the chain of command. This is an activity called discipline, and is unpopular. Perhaps true accountability and budget forces will do the trick. But I doubt it.

Another aspect that should be looked at closely is language. I know that English is an (or the) international language, but most meetings involving Europeans are accomplished through the extensive use of interpreters. There are good and bad interpreters. Some are inexperienced, others are bored but competent, yet others are difficult to understand because all normal emphasis is missing; only a few are brilliant. Even 'simultaneous' interpreting is a sequential activity; the time-lag destroys much spontaneity and even the most brilliant interpreters have a speed limit often below that of an excited French delegate. Misunderstandings arise. With Americans too, we are divided by language, although it is possible to work through without interpreters. The American language is full of jargon of the wrong sort and invented words and phrases that really irritate, such as 'verbal interface meeting' for discussion, and 'make me smart on this thing' instead of enlighten me. But Americans also have a wealth of wonderful expressions. A selection of those recorded by British delegations include:

> *Assume makes an ASS out of YOU and ME*
> *What we got here is an elephant we gonna have to stack in this bitty paper bag. (Apropos the difficulty of fitting a transceiver design in the space available.)*
> *What we got here is two tons of fertilizer in a one-ton truck. (Apropos the same problem.)*
> *On a scale of one to ten, I'll give that twelve.*
> *Nobody's shot in the arse with this proposal. (A puzzled European asked: Is that good or bad?)*
> *The man that does the most work, makes the most mistakes.*[1]

The important thing is that Americans use these expressions, whether they are spontaneous inspirations or traditional sayings; many colourful British expressions used by our grandparents are fast disappearing and being replaced by grey, hackneyed, forgettable prose.

There is little we can do to replace interpreters now, although in time it may be possible to ensure that all British engineers and managers have a reasonable grounding in French and German. I am told that all German engineers learn English as a full engineering subject. At a week-long meeting on a high-tech project I found it remarkable that two German engineers, who had been given three hours to cover the details of the processor to a multinational audience, spoke in perfect English with hardly an accent for two hours 59 minutes and covered the complex engineering detail most clearly. They were not specially brought-in linguists but the engineers designing the processor. The British and Americans hardly bother with foreign languages, falling back rather comfortably on the notion that 'they' all understand and speak English. This irritates foreigners, especially Frenchmen, which does not surprise me. If we cannot compete with them, we ought to show willing and learn to speak reasonable social French and German. It should not be left to individuals to learn languages in their own time: they should be taught at the staff college or other courses.

We must recognise the irritant to others. I had dinner many years ago with a Dutch air force officer. He spent part of the meal seriously proposing the use of Esperanto as the only official language in NATO committees and panels. This surprised me – like most Dutchmen, he was a brilliant linguist. He explained, however, that even he found it difficult at times in NATO panels to understand complex arguments in English or French, the only official NATO languages. He claimed that as a result, British, French, American, Canadian and some Belgian delegates had a major advantage over the others who were not using their mother tongue. Esperanto would put everyone at the same disadvantage! He failed to acknowledge my view that this was a levelling down, not a levelling up, and that the first four of the above nations tended to do all the written work in and out of committee, a chore all would have to share if Esperanto took over. Nevertheless, he had a point. We ought to soothe this irritant a little. At least we know the French, Germans and other Europeans: many American industrialists are not sure whether Scotland is in England or Europe is in London, and the whole concepts of Great Britain and the United Kingdom are beyond them. Shaw and Wilde, if they have heard of them, are of course 'Englishmen'.

Language may be a side issue. Costs are not. Costs are often cited as the reason we cannot afford not to collaborate. This seems dubious to me. Production costs can indeed be lower, but not as much as many proponents of collaboration claim: five per cent lower might be a reasonable estimate. National development costs should be lower but overall costs are in fact higher, so the national share is not as low as often claimed. In-Service running costs are likely to be much the same. There are some savings, but they are not massive. Against this must be set the higher costs of the longer time span of a collaborative programme, particularly where more than two nations are involved. If a national development programme takes ten years, an international programme might take 15 years. Time is money.

I am not convinced by the fashionable argument that collaboration is financially essential, except for some low-volume high-tech equipment. Neither am I convinced that we must all have the same equipment to make fighting with our allies more effective. This is a much more persuasive argument than the financial one, but it needs to be broken down. For instance, it makes little difference if we all have different bayonets or even different small arms. There is, however, a strong argument for having common equipment where we have to interoperate above brigade level. Communications, command and control, surveillance and target acquisition equipment all need to be common. Large equipment with very many components, even if used exclusively at brigade level or below, should also be common where possible for repair and maintenance reasons. Munitions should all be compatible with each other's platforms. The difficulties of achieving these aims are immense; but the rewards in war are significant. Collaboration with our major allies at all levels is the only way to achieve it.

'Excuse me, General, are you intending to attend the two-week symposium on "General Purpose, Optimistic, Parallel Discrete-Event Simulators Based on Object Oriented Methodology" in Venice next month? You are? Good! Then I shall accompany you. Which experts would you like to have along to help you with the papers, and who would you like to help you with your bags? Thank you. I'll make the arrangements.'

'It's alright for some!', I hear you say.

Soliloquy on Life and Death
(Hamlet, Act III, Scene 1)
US Department of Defence Version

ঽ▲

To maintain survivalship or to transition to negative survivalship is a critical issue for addressing in evaluation mode at this point in time.

Whether a more positive resolution is to establish a passive compliance matrix, despite quasi-terminal engagement by low technology missiles, or to rescope and transition to effective retaliatory mode, is an upcoming moot point.

To transition to irreversible passive mode, with the mission of initiating resolution of the negative robustness of the presently form-factored, animate confi- guration has a stomach feel consonant with meeting current evaluation criteria.

The prospect of fully-powered-down status, with a non-zero probability of expe- riencing unconstrained manifestations of bio-imagery, indicates the desirability of entering a holding mode.

This carries greater weight than the sum of a number of initially envisioned evalu- ation criteria, including bio-degradatory activity, responsivity to oppression, contumeliousness, amatorial non-reciprocity, temporal adequacy of legal compli- ance, and fardel poundage.

In summation: evaluatory cognitive processes are indicative of higher technical risk. The trade-off between current mission configurations and those which can- not be evaluated with specific certainty in the context of the innovative, higher entropy, build standard is indicative of reversion to the existing solution.

N.B. I am indebted to David Redman for drawing this translation to my attention.

PART TWO
SOME SOLUTIONS

CHAPTER TEN
The Defence Costs Study – A Wasted Opportunity

Army loses OK Corral bunfight.
HEADLINE IN THE TIMES, 16 JULY 1994

The Defence Costs Study, or 'Front Line First' as it was called for public relations purposes, had its roots in Options for Change, which was discussed briefly in an earlier chapter. Options for Change was a hurried exercise, carried out in a strategic and tactical vacuum, to find a set level of 'peace dividend' savings apparently to satisfy the demand of ordinary people for something in return for Cold War victory. In fact, such a public demand did not really exist, even if some sections of the media presented it that way. What did exist was a demand from the Treasury for large and early savings. This was not to be denied, or even opposed.

Options for Change was a hurried, inept affair. John Keegan, in a 1990 article in *The Daily Telegraph* , wrote:

What has been done so far has been done with the greatest ineptitude ... Options for Change is a misnomer. It really meant Options for Avoiding Trouble. The calculation was that the regimental officers, being gentlemen, would bite the bullet and go quietly ... 'Smaller but bitter' is the paraphrase of the Ministry's 'Smaller but better' that is circulating.

Even in the absence of a new NATO strategy and guidance from the Cabinet on the future role and tasks of the armed forces, the result stands out as grossly illogical. While MOD was to take 20 per cent cuts and some areas, for example Intelligence, none at all, the Army was to be cut by 25 per cent, the Royal Armoured Corps by 42 per cent, the Royal Artillery by 27 per cent and the Infantry by 35 per cent. In the same article, Keegan pointed out: 'In the last resort, the worth of an Army is calculated in the number of infantry battalions and armoured regiments that it can field.' By this reckoning, Options for Change reduced the Army by an amount approaching 40 per cent while the huge management and administrative overhead was reduced by less than 20 per cent. The ratio of 'front-line' to 'support' was therefore lowered drastically . Keegan again:

Britain is about to have its Army cut to below a level which is safe for national defence.

Options for Change was carried out in very strict secrecy, with only those with a 'need to know' having access to what was going on. Inevitably some information leaked out and caused considerable apprehension, heightened by the absolute lack of any official statement or announcement, either public or in a more restricted way to the armed forces and other defence workers. It was clear that there would be major redundancies, but where would the axe fall? Everyone felt his or her career was on the line. Morale plummeted. In July 1990, six months after the Options for Change work had begun, the Secretary of State for Defence made a statement in the House. It lacked detail and only had the effect of deepening the gloom. The Army was to be cut drastically, but how was not clear. The other two services were hit less heavily but hard enough, and the same gloom enveloped them. Eight days later, Saddam Hussein invaded Kuwait.

The Gulf War had two effects on morale. First there was an immediate and steep rise as all those involved, and to a lesser extent those not involved, felt pride and a sense of achievement in the Army's action, culminating in the brilliant victory. As time went on, however, this euphoria was tempered by the realisation that the deployment of one division, and a weak one at that, was stretching the Army far more than had been anticipated. The simultaneous deployment of two divisions would have been impossible. Put beside the US force, the UK contribution, although magnified by the media out of all recognition, was tiny. On the world scene, at least at the high-intensity end, the British army was hardly a major player any longer.

There was a little misplaced optimism that the Gulf War would do for the Army what the Falklands did for the Navy in the immediate aftermath of Nott's review. This optimism was not to last for long. In a *Financial Times* article in March 1991, David White wrote:

> *But while the Gulf crisis has delayed decisions on UK defence cuts, the overall framework of the government's plans appears unlikely to alter. Indeed it has become apparent that the money available under the MOD's 'long term costings' (classified figures covering the next 10 years) may not even stretch to cover the reduced armed forces structure foreseen under the plan.*

Options for Change rolled forward to a post-Options Army which will have difficulty in sustaining more than one all-arms brigade in the field with the necessary backup. We have far fewer tanks and artillery pieces than any of the 14 major CSE nations and far fewer than many third world military powers. The following figures speak for themselves:

Table 2
Tank and Artillery Holdings 1995

Country	Tanks	Artillery	Defence Expenditure (US $bn)
United Kingdom	666	544	34.2
Turkey	2,608	3,125	6.0
Spain	630	1,210	8.5
Netherlands	734	580	8.5
Italy	1,164	1,939	20.0
Greece	1,735	1,878	5.1
Germany	3,032	2,056	41.8
France	1,289	1,251	48.0
Bulgaria	1,475	1,750	0.4
Poland	1,721	1,581	2.6
Romania	1,375	1,471	0.9
Pakistan	2,050	1,820	3.8
India	3,500	4,355	8.3
South Korea	2,050	4,500	15.6
Vietnam	1,300	2,300	1.0
Algeria	960	906	1.2
Egypt	4,850	4,003	2.4
Iran	1,440	2,948	3.4
Israel	4,300	1,650	7.2
Libya	2,210	1,870	1.4
Syria	4,600	2,560	2.0

Note: All figures taken from *The Military Balance*, published for the International Institute for Strategic Studies, Oxford University Press, London (1996).

I have already quoted David Hart in Chapter Five on the ratio of generals to total Army servicemen, but it is perhaps worth repeating that, according to his findings, we have quite an extraordinary number of senior officers compared with other nations, the ratio of British general officers to total servicemen being 1:420, compared to the 1:1,900 in the USA and France or 1:2,300 in Germany.

The phrase 'not enough bang for our bucks' has obviously become a true reflection of our armed forces. We may have the best fighting men in the world and we may train them and lead them better than any other nation, but they are not going to be effective if they have to operate against a sophisticated enemy in too small numbers and with too little prime fighting equipment.

It would be comforting to think that the Defence Costs Study was a direct result of lessons learned from Options for Change and the Gulf War, but it was not. It arose from the inability to fund the Options programme without yet more significant damage, as was predicted by White in the above quote. The shortfall amounted to more than £1bn in the first three years and £1bn per year thereafter across the ten-year long-term costing period (and presumably beyond), or £8bn in the costing period: a very large sum. That the Defence Costs Study was, like Options for Change, finance-driven, is clear from the MOD report by the House of Commons Defence Committee which states:

The Defence Costs Study was undertaken in direct response to the level of defence expenditure agreed in the 1993 Public Expenditure Survey. On 30 November 1993 the Chancellor of the Exchequer announced that defence expenditure would be set very substantially below the level which had been assumed ... The next day, the Secretary of State, in oral evidence to this committee announced the establishment of the Defence Costs Study.[1]

More cuts in defence for financial reasons would have been extremely harmful to public perceptions. The bad news was camouflaged by presenting this exercise as a quest for greater efficiency:

There is a continuing need to ensure that the administration and support of our armed forces are subjected to the most rigorous analysis. Only by doing that can we ensure that the money available for defence is being spent properly, and in a way which contributes to our fighting capability.[2]

This was to be welcomed. While it would have been better to carry out the Defence Costs Study to achieve savings in the tail to spend on the teeth, there was much to be said for a major exercise to find a shortfall in funding from the support areas without touching front-line units. In fact, it should be asked why this had not been done before. Year after year we have had to find savings, often of an enormous amount, just to balance the books for another year. Year after year, the same salami-slicing tactics have been used to emasculate the same areas, particularly training levels and equipment procurement.

'Let us do things properly', was the fairly general and genuine feeling. There was certainly much that needed subjecting to detailed scrutiny. There were to be no sacred cows. As the Secretary of State put it, we must not 'let sentimental attachment to traditional ways of doing things override our prime purpose'.[3] According to the Permanent Under Secretary, Sir Christopher France, the Defence Costs Study was 'an opportunity for achieving better value in the way we do business'.[4]

'Doing things properly' in a big organisation requires tough, high-level decisions, but also a knowledgeable, wide-angle view across the whole. The Defence Costs Study needed such a view to come to some initial decisions on the most fundamental issues (organisational and procedural) before passing them down as guidelines for the more detailed work. It needed the most senior officers, military and civilian, to earn their salaries. But no such overall view was apparently taken and the initiating instructions for the study were left to the Costs Review Secretariat, which was headed jointly by one Air Vice Marshal and one Assistant Under Secretary. There was no way in which they could have imposed their own changes to top-level structure in areas headed by 5-star officers.

As a result, the top-level groups waited for ideas to surface from the individual study teams that had been set up to examine certain areas in detail. Each study team was therefore working in a vacuum and liable to come up with recommendations which clashed fundamentally with those from other teams. Although the Executive Group and the Costs Review Secretariat were to exert co-ordinating functions, the lack of a clear overall plan was a serious flaw. Given time, this flaw could have been eliminated, albeit at the expense of large and nugatory efforts as teams were sent back to square one. But time was not on offer. The Secretary of State's announcement to the House of Commons was made on 1 December 1993, and it was mid-December before the study teams were set up, tasked and manned. Reports on emerging findings were to be produced by mid-February, which seems long enough, but here bureaucracy and the need for consultation took over. The upshot was that the individual study reports were to be completed by the first week in January. Some teams got little more than four or five working days to consider, study and evaluate the most complex issues, such as in one procurement field the advantages of leasing or contractorising transport, the level of stock holdings and the need to balance warning times against procurement lead times, reliance on commercial standards, possible multi-equipment procurement deals, packaging standards and so on. Not a suitable task for a few working days just prior to Christmas.

The compressed time scale, which probably went unnoticed at the top, combined with the lack of any firm high-level plan, constituted a serious weakness which was to show itself, in due course, in the almost total disaster of some of the

individual studies. But these few were important ones; others were less affected.

One novel feature of the early period was a call for individuals to forward their own ideas. Regrettably, they were processed through the chain of command and many radical ideas were weeded out early or simply not put forward at all. This exercise resulted in thousands of suggestions, varying from major proposals to abolish the post of Chief of Defence Procurement, to abandon the move of the Procurement Executive to Abbey Wood and to get rid of the MOD headquarters' IT system CHOTS, to small ideas such as to dig up the grass round MOD property and plant vegetables. Whether many of these ideas were seriously considered is doubtful as the teams had already been tasked, but no doubt some were added in. At the very least it was a good PR and management exercise.

Many people were enthusiastic about getting the Defence Costs Study right, but some were despondent and some downright hostile. I remember someone's farewell drinks party just before that Christmas at which I heard some pretty vicious remarks from very senior civil servants who were incensed that their cosy little world was going to be looked at. Later they were to do a good job of repelling would-be boarders, and the mandarins got away almost scot-free.

There was plenty of enthusiasm, though, in the early days and considerable confidence that the exercise would be constructive and beneficial. Many believed that sacred cows would be slaughtered by the dozen, that unnecessary bureaucracy would be heaped on the rubbish dump, and that greater efficiency through proper delegation would be achieved. Even I, an apparent cynic, believed that much was achievable, but I was doubtful whether the will existed at high level to reform the Main Building organisation and procedures that lay at the heart of MOD inefficiency. I was of course interested primarily in those individual studies that affected equipment procurement, and I pointed out to a Defence Manufacturers Association seminar in March 1994:

> *I believe the study will have failed if the changes proposed are not radical ... such a failure will not only rebound on the equipment programme but also perpetuate the lack of accountability which weakens the whole structure ... we must get the big issues right, but will we?*

The initial enthusiasm waned as the first months of 1994 drew on. After the early involvement of large numbers of military and civilian desk officers, complete silence descended as the higher-level study teams and the Executive Group considered the interim proposals. What leaked out was less than encouraging: it seemed that major cuts, many of them long overdue, were being considered in a large number of areas. They would have significant effects on a great number of servicemen and even civilians. But it also began to appear that the really big issues, those of accountability and unnecessary bureaucracy, were being fudged. Uncertainty over the future, already high as Options for Change worked its way through, increased, and morale suffered. These are some examples from a Preview article on morale in the Procurement Executive:

> *Very low – people feel trapped and outsiders don't want to come in. – EO London.*
> *I have been in MOD for 30 years and never known it as bad as it is now. – HPTO London.*
> *Morale is low because of all the uncertainties. There is a lot of suspicion that we are not being told everything. – HEO Bath.*
> *Uncertainty about the future, and relocation, means morale is pretty low. There doesn't seem to be much communication from higher management. – EO London.*
> *Very low indeed. Change and disruption have had an effect and people feel they are not considered before things are decided. – EO Glasgow.*[5]

My concern was the progress of those studies which would affect equipment procurement. There were four: DCS 1, which looked at MOD headquarters' organisation and procedures; DCS 4, which looked at science and technology; DCS 5, which investigated procurement practices; and DCS 6, which examined organisation of procurement. At an early stage it appeared that DCS 5 had little to say and that DCS 1 and DCS 4 were deliberately kept so vague that they were unlikely to produce useful outputs.

In contrast, DCS 6 was a real winner, or so it seemed. John Chisholm, a cool, logical, objective man, had struck at the heart of the problem – lack of accountability. His study was a model of excellence, exhibiting a clear vision and an attention to detail which put to shame the shoddy work in other studies. Here was the salvation of the Defence Costs Study in terms of equipment procurement.

This was progress but Chisholm had gone outside his rather narrow remit, which he had to if he was to tackle the subject properly as most of the problem lay in the constraints imposed by Main Building procedures. His report contained proposals which radically affected DCS 1 and upset the mandarins, whose role and power was to be curtailed severely while that of the military was to be increased. It was also proposed that the Procurement Executive should become a strict supplier, losing much of its influence and many staff. This no doubt upset the Chief of Defence Procurement (CDP). Chisholm's proposals had raised powerful opposition. Could he win? In the end he did not – DCS 6 was marginalised, and the same level of savings as Chisholm had proposed were to be found, without saying how, by the Procurement Executive. The outlook was now bleak.

What was needed was a wholesale change to bring in proper accountability, which means both responsibility and power, and this could only be done by major changes in culture throughout MOD. It could not come about through changes of interface, reorganisation and tinkering at the margins with procedures. Yet this is what the Defence Costs Study left us with.

This is perhaps not surprising as no-one at the top understood equipment procurement in enough depth to recognise the worth of Chisholm's work, nor to understand the penalty of ditching and replacing it with marginal, vague tinkering with the status quo. One only has to look at the composition of the Steering Group and Executive Group to see that neither the Secretary of State nor the Minister (Defence Procurement) got expert advice in this field. There was CDP but it seems that he was committed to the move to Abbey Wood of a largely unchanged Procurement Executive. If he was not, either he failed to appreciate the problems or he was ignored.

There was of course a reason why the other members on these top-level groups should pay scant attention to procurement: media interest. Having heard the Defence Costs Study billed as a major efficiency exercise to restore balance between the front line and the rear, an exercise in which there were to be no sacred cows, the media were only interested in the latter aspect. Procurement hardly fell into this category. Royal Air Force manning did, as did joint headquarters, Navy infrastructure, training and manning, the Territorial Army, and many of the smaller issues such as bands, animals, messes and chaplains. Arcane procedures in the Main Building or the Procurement Executive were unlikely to ignite the media or cause much excitement in the Services at large. Given the lack of knowledge at the top and the uninterest of all but a very small minority, it was hardly surprising if procurement was patted on the head and allowed to amble back to its lair.

What were the problems that Defence Costs Studies 1 and 6 should have tackled? Nothing more than those identified in earlier chapters. Above all lay the problem of lack of accountability. Those charged with identifying requirements and developing equipment to meet them had enormous responsibility but little power. At full colonel or assistant director level, these people had to seek authority at every turn not only from their immediate bosses, or their bosses' bosses, but also from a host of onlookers who had no responsibility but the enormous power of the absolute veto. The whole edifice of procurement organisation and procedure was built upon this divide between responsibility and authority. Individuals were powerless to identify who did well and who deserved the sack. How could a hopeless manager be sacked if he had no real power to get things done? The mediocre and worse clogged the procurement machine.

One aspect of this problem was financial. Not only was there a lack of financial delegation, but those responsible overall had no financial authority at the highest level. The arrangements for financial delegation within the procurement field would not have been applauded by Alice had they been recited by the March Hare at the Mad Hatter's tea party. They can be briefly stated thus: Funds are put into the programme for a new project by the consensus of a wide range of people. Some individuals, who have no responsibility for the end result, can remove them without consensus. The equipment requirement has to be agreed by the high-level Equipment Approvals Committee but can only reach them after widespread scrutiny and consensus, as the director responsible for the requirement has no real authority on his own. The Equipment Approvals Committee agrees the requirement and approves the funding which is then passed not to the author of the requirement but direct to the Procurement Executive. The Procurement Executive can spend this money how it wishes, subject to a million-and-one checks, balances, scrutinies and delays, but only so long as the funding is not removed arbitrarily by the individuals referred to above. The Procurement Executive can spend but is not responsible for ensuring that the equipment is eventually suitable for deployment in the field. This is the responsibility of the original Requirements branch, which has no power over how the development money is spent.

So if a £500m project is found to be unsuitable for deployment and the contract is not strong enough to get industry to pay to put it right, whose fault is it? The answer is: the MOD's. It cannot be traced to one individual, either high or low, or even to one committee or collective decision. Unless the equipment is shut in a garage and left to rot, more money has to be found from a hard-pressed budget. Who in MOD would really care? Unless of course a sleuth from the tabloid press or the House of Commons Defence Committee was on the trail.

These issues should have been grasped and dealt with. Under Chisholm's proposals they would have been. In their wisdom, the top people ignored them. Too many sacred cows roamed at will.

With Chisholm's DCS 6 kicked firmly into touch, the MOD headquarters DCS 1 was left free to concentrate on superficialities. On the final list of agreed DCS 1 measures, I annotated six of them as 'superficial', one as 'very superficial', one as 'minor', two as a 'fudge' and the remaining one as irrelevant to procurement. To give you some idea of its level, one of the ten measures was: 'Director General Management Audit (DGMA) to be retitled Director General Management and Organisation (DGMO).' There were some changes for the better in DCS 1, but they failed to tackle the real issues and most did not affect equipment. The improvements were therefore of marginal benefit to procurement.

If DCS 1 and DCS 6 were finally of minor achievement, they probably did nothing to make matters significantly worse. They did find some savings and if that was all the Defence Costs Study was about, I suppose they achieved their aim. Not so DCS 4, which looked at Science and Technology. This study proposed savings that had little basis in logic. There were a few good points, not least the incorporation of the remaining research establishments into one agency with the Defence Research Agency. This would be a good thing if the new agency could get rid of its lumbering management and procedures overheads to give full value for money. But elsewhere it was a disaster, as it all added up to cuts in research spending. They masqueraded under headings such as 'rationalisation' and 'not required for the future equipment programme', but the result was a massive cut (around 25 per cent) in our already pitifully inadequate research spending. Although the scientists seemed little concerned, the military, who directed the applied research programme, were horrified. Even if the proposed cuts were made, they would come nowhere near delivering the total of savings calculated without either reducing the ability of the customer to direct the programme or making further cuts in the research programme. DCS 4 was a disaster which need not have happened.

Predictably, neither science and technology nor procurement organisation featured as issues when the Secretary of State announced the Defence Costs Study findings in July 1994. Sweetened by commitment to a number of new equipment programmes (some of which had been announced before and others had been specially 'saved up'), the package was well camouflaged and well presented. Not surprisingly, the media concentrated on the man and the Services rather than on MOD procedures, with newspaper headlines shouting:

Staff squeeze empties 20 London buildings
Tories in marginal seats face backlash over defence cuts
Curbs in service rivalry
How the RAF fought to the last desk
RAF to lose 7,500 jobs
Marines' music school that beat the IRA to be closed
Service chiefs take bitter pill

18,000 jobs go
Army loses OK Corral bunfight

Under the last headline, Simon Jenkins wrote in *The Times* of 16 July 1994:

Something is amiss. This week a 5 per cent cut was made to Britain's defence bud-
get and everybody said it was 'about right'. Retired admirals, armchair generals,
even Tory defence spokesmen such as Sir Nicholas Bonsor lined up to declare the
cuts 'no threat to national security'. It was steady as she goes. I draw one of two
conclusions from this wimpish response. Either the cuts did not go far enough, or
Britain's armed forces have lost their will to fight. Both are equally alarming.

The armed forces actually had lost the fight the previous November when the
Chancellor announced a reduction in the defence budget. Given this, the outcome
of the Defence Costs Study was not another fight lost but a successful limitation on
the damage that could have been caused by the defeat in 1993. In that context, it was
a major success. By taking the four to five per cent cut without touching the front
line posed 'no threat to national security'. This is why in July 1994 retired admirals
and armchair generals were supportive. Anything else would have been another
defeat.

But Jenkins was right in his other conclusion. The cuts did not go far enough. Large areas which were ripe for a major overhaul escaped largely untouched or even with their numbers enhanced. MOD in particular remained a bloated dinosaur. If MOD had been sensible, it would have used the immediate aftermath for a quiet revolution while there was no political will for further cuts. There were still huge opportunities for increasing the Services' teeth at the expense not so much of the tail but of the useless overheads. The brief honeymoon is now over: defence is back on the chopping-block. I suspect that MOD will lack the will to do anything further until forced: the telescope to the blind eye can be so useful.

CHAPTER ELEVEN

Making Accountability Work

Power without responsibility –
the prerogative of the harlot throughout the ages.
RUDYARD KIPLING, CONVERSATION WITH MAX AITKIN

The first part of this book has produced a lot of evidence of the weaknesses that exist in MOD and their implications for equipment procurement. They produce major delays, gross overmanning, poor decisions and low morale, all of which can be translated into huge increases in costs. Something must obviously be done. The Defence Costs Study made some efforts but although it produced much that was welcome, it missed the boat. It is much easier to criticise than to propose sensible solutions that will work, and this may be why the Defence Costs Study overall failed. Part Two of this book will address the difficult bit and propose many changes to resolve the deficiencies. It will stand or fall on how well it does so.

The first, and much the most important issue is that of accountability. Without successful change here, nothing much will be achieved apart from a certain amount of fiddling at the edges giving an illusion of progress. Achieving proper accountability is the first step to much greater progress. I believe that it is not an overstatement to say that there is currently no true accountability and that until this changes, the glaring deficiencies will remain. Avoiding the issue condemns us to continued overmanning, underperformance and muddled decision-making.

It is obvious that we need to retain some system of checks so that mistakes can be avoided or at least detected before too much time has elapsed. But there must be a much more sensible balance between the delay such checks impose and the risk taken. Time is money also in procurement, so delays are very costly. Increased risk is not always as costly. The trick is to match the two.

The first and biggest change that has to be made is the matching of responsibility and authority. Far too many people in the MOD procurement world have immense responsibility but little real authority to discharge it; conversely there are far too many people with immense authority (particularly the authoritative veto) and no responsibility for the end result. Embodying authority, including proper financial delegation, within the same post as the responsibility would lead immediately to quicker decisions, made by those who know the facts, together with a complete responsibility for those decisions. With the right person in the job these decisions would be at least as good as any committee decisions taken now, and often better.

Starting at the top, there must be one person responsible for all aspects of deploying force. This has to be the Chief of the Defence Staff. Directly responsible to him are the Chiefs of Staff for each service. Unless their responsibility includes that of fielding future equipment, they cannot be fully responsible for deploying force, and accountability lies nowhere. To many people this is just plain common sense and has been advocated time and again. In the early 1980s, Brian Taylor wrote:

> *The PE could become a fifth wheel on the MOD coach ... the ultimate home of Service procurement, although a specialised management activity, is arguably back under the Service Boards. There is nothing inevitable about a separate procurement organisation.*[1]

More recently, Chisholm came to much the same conclusion in his initial work in the Defence Costs Study. Such a change would seemingly set back 'purple-isation'. But is this on its own a strong enough argument to overcome a move to proper accountability? No, of course not.

Each Chief of Staff would need a 'Chief of Procurement' directly responsible to him or her. For the Army, this officer could be called the Master General of the Ordnance (a post dating back to 1414), but he would be responsible, at 3-star level, for all aspects of Army systems procurement, including research, requirement, development, production and fielding. In other words, he would amalgamate the responsibilities of the present MGO and the Assistant Chief of the Defence Staff (Operational Requirements) (ACDS OR). There would no longer be split responsibilities between the staff requirement and the technical specification, or between those and project funding, currently largely the titular responsibility of the Army and actually the responsibility of Central Staffs.

Having amalgamated MGO and ACDS OR(Land), it follows that the role of project manager must be amalgamated with the Operational Requirements branch head to produce one individual with the clear responsibility of writing the technical specification to reflect the military need. He or she would work for the new Army Chief of Procurement, MGO, and not the Chief of Defence Procurement. Of necessity, they would bring across to Whitehall a substantial slice of their project staff, leaving behind only those who are necessary to do the nuts and bolts of procurement such as writing contracts and checking milestones against contracts, quality control and property rights. The Procurement Executive would no longer be an executive but a much smaller agency. These changes would ensure that at each level there was one person with the overall responsibility. They must also be given the authority: all those people with a powerful veto but no responsibility must be cleared away.

There would be no place for the current sort of scrutiny. This will be a terrifying thought for many people: how on earth can we trust an individual? Of course we cannot. The best individual will make mistakes and a few, very few on current evidence, may bend the rules unacceptably. However, the extra trust and responsibility reposed in that individual will almost always motivate him to do his best. But if that best is not good enough and if that individual is clearly accountable for his decisions, it must be possible to call him to account later. This means that scrutiny must be retained, but generally after the decision instead of before it.

What is needed is in-depth audit at intervals, placed sensibly to catch mistakes before too much damage is done, but infrequent enough to cause little delay. These audits should be linked to high-level committee decisions or to specific break points in the development of the project. Instead of the scores of superficial scrutiny exercises that currently take place during ten years of development, there should perhaps be no more than half-a-dozen during that time or even less. One audit would take place to launch the project at the beginning of the current pre-feasibility stage, with emphasis on maturity of research, early prototyping, risk, operational analysis, the military requirement and future concepts. Another at the start of what is now Project Definition 2, with emphasis on the military requirement, programme costs, long-term value for money and contractual conditions. One more at the end of development prior to the authorisation of production, with emphasis on production costs, achievement of contractual development and fitness for purpose. And no more than three (and preferably fewer) at other points during development depending on its form and the size of project. They would be conducted by teams including experts in finance, contracts, project management, technical issues and user requirements, last for about a week, and discuss the detailed findings with the accountable official before publication to ensure that all misunderstandings are eliminated. The aim would be to pick up major errors, to change direction only where essential, and to authorise continuance to the top procurement committee as quickly as possible. The audit report would not be circulated for comment; it would be agreed with the individual responsible for that project (or points of disagreement clearly laid out) and passed direct to the Equipment Approvals Committee for endorsement.

With the right person in the job and the knowledge that in-depth audits, rather than the current 'tick-in-the-box' approach, will probe every move in due course, the results should be satisfactory and the risks not increased. Indeed risks might very well be reduced. Such an approach would demand longer tours for key individuals. A project manager should be expected to serve for the life of the project from the start of pre-feasibility to the end of development. Currently this could be anything from ten to twenty years, but with the changes proposed above it could be reduced drastically to about six to ten years. Even this is a long time for a competent, ambitious person – which in turn suggests promotion in post for success. At the moment this happens with a few of the technical project managers, but not at all with military ones. If the audit is the stick, the carrot is in-post promotion. Those that do not measure up will not get promotion; those that fail will be sacked at the first hurdle.

Such an approach would lead to the elimination of many 'scrutineers' and hangers-on. Some could be re-deployed to a central audit team under the aegis of the Permanent Under Secretary, others could be removed from the payroll. Moreover, as project managers currently spend some 80 per cent of their time not managing their projects, the proposed changes would almost quintuple the time they can spend on their projects; similarly their staff. As a result, day-to-day decisions would be quicker, management of projects more effective, the need for consultants less and the ability to reduce staff increased. All this could save large sums; halving the period of the development cycle, for example, would reduce development costs by 20 to 40 per cent and would reduce production costs by a somewhat smaller percentage, but a smaller percentage of a much larger amount. It is difficult to quantify the cost of delay accurately, but it is interesting that a report by the National Audit Office on the British Library attributes £50m (or ten per cent of the total costs) to delays in the first phase alone.[2]

I recently asked a senior industrialist his recipe for success (yes, there are successful industrial firms). He replied that it lay in the authority and responsibility given to the project managers. They are the most important people in the company and all other company employees, whether 'below' or 'above' them, exist to support them. The project manager was king. MOD needs to embrace this approach, but it is a long way from the current situation. The thought that the Chief of Defence Procurement, the Principal Director of Contracts and the assistant under secretaries exist to support the project managers is a long way, I believe, from their view of the situation. Yet this is the way to go.

This principle can be extended to other areas in the equipment world, notably Operational Requirements. The branch head, who is already responsible for requirements and the overall equipment programme in his area, should be given the commensurate authority to go with it. So should the superintendents of research. It should be noted that I have pitched the level of this accountability at the project manager/Operational Requirements branch head; that is, at about full colonel or assistant director level. It needs to be at that level because below it individuals will have too little experience, and above it they will be responsible for too wide an area to be involved in the day-to-day decision-making. Promotion in post, where advisable, would be to brigadier or director.

To sum up: the key to improvement throughout the equipment procurement world within MOD is the delegation of authority, including financial authority, to match an individual's responsibility. This will achieve clear accountability. To make it effective, there must be an end to 'tick-in-the-box' scrutiny and the institution of in-depth audits at a frequency of at least three, and no more than six times during the development of a project, from the start of pre-feasibility to the end of full development. These audits will assess decision in retrospect, not in prospect, so that the responsible individuals no longer have to refer day-to-day decisions up and sideways to a myriad of veto merchants before they can go forward. The responsible individuals, even if they delegate, remain accountable. They must be selected from those with the right training, background and expertise and they must remain in post for the whole development cycle, being promoted if successful, or not if unsuccessful. If they are found to be not up to the job, they must be removed at once. These individuals are the key to success. They must be supported by those above and below them and must be allowed to get on with day-to-day management without interference. Such a change would not only eliminate the need for many of today's 'scrutineers' and hangers-on, but would greatly speed up project development, thereby saving large sums of money. It is the fundamental starting point if we are at all serious about providing value for money in procurement.

CHAPTER TWELVE

Introducing Professionalism

An' it all goes into the laundry,
But it never comes out in the wash,
'Ow we're sugared about by the old men
('Eavy-sterned amateur old men!)
That 'amper and 'inder an' scold men ...
RUDYARD KIPLING, STELLENBOSCH

In Chapter Seven, I quoted the Chief of Defence Procurement's view that the Procurement Executive is a highly professional outfit, but went on to show that both outsiders and those inside believe that it is bureaucratic, unresponsive and inflexible, that it is not organised for effective management, that accountability is blurred, and that its staff lacks knowledge. In other words, there is a deficiency of professionalism in the Procurement Executive which is particularly notable in the areas of project management, cost management and contract writing. Some, but certainly not all of the blame can be laid at the door of MOD and the attitudes and procedures in Whitehall. It is imperative that MOD as a whole becomes more professional in its equipment dealings, whether it is the scientist, the accountant, the military or the project manager. The current amateurism right across the board has to end.

The changes proposed in the last chapter are the cornerstone; without them, we are condemned to remain distinctly amateur. But this is not the whole story, and in this chapter I will propose changes to introduce professionalism on the assumption that the following proposals are implemented: proper accountability is introduced, authority goes hand-in-hand with responsibility, tenures are increased with promotion for the successful and the sack for the less than highly competent, and in-depth but infrequent audit replaces the 'tick-in-the-box' children's game that currently passes for scrutiny. A mighty big assumption, you will say, and so it is. But without these changes, others will be ineffective.

The most serious charge is that of lack of expertise, knowledge and experience. This must be tolerated no longer. There is far too much movement between areas with the result that project managers and their staffs, operational requirements and concepts staff, financial and contracts personnel and others have little real knowledge of the details which are essential to day-to-day management and lack the necessary background and historical knowledge.

Longer tenures, which is a base assumption of this chapter, will enable the post-holder to build up expertise and knowledge in a particular area. This is essential as longer tenures mean fewer posts over a set number of years. These posts must all be in related areas to ensure the maximum build-up of expertise so as to match that of industry and enable the post-holder to develop the ability to conduct 'robust', but knowledgeable, discussions not only when he has been in post for several months but throughout his tour. It is surely unacceptable for key managers to be feeling their way for the first six months (perhaps 25 per cent) of their term. Taken over a decade, this 'down-time' for a change of project manager every two years or so amounts to two and a half years. With tenures of up to ten years, this 'down-time' would be negligible.

Some people will say that this would narrow their experience so much that they would never become effective top managers. That is a flawed argument. Quite apart from the fact that most recent holders of the posts of Chief of Defence Procurement and Master General of the Ordnance have come from outside the equipment procurement world, directors and directors general tend to deal only with high-level, and generally common, problems. Provided they are supported by (or better support) expert project managers, they will be effective. Without that expertise, they will continue to dwell on relatively minor management issues and to safeguard perks rather than grasp the really prickly problems.

Longer tenures, greater knowledge and more time provided by much less scrutiny of the kind described in earlier chapters will enable MOD to improve its appalling record on learning by experience. A project manager in post for ten years, with his promotion determined by success, will not make the same mistake twice. He will try not to make that mistake at all by delving into mistakes and practices in other areas. Higher management might require managers to contribute to a central living document on the subject instead of allowing mistakes to go unrecorded or, if they are recorded occasionally, to gather dust unread on some shelf unknown to others.

I doubt if motivation will remain a problem with the added authority and accountability, and with promotion in the balance – at least for the most competent. If the less competent go elsewhere it is not to be decried. The rewards must at least balance the burdens, however, or many of the most competent people may also choose to leave. Promotion and power are two powerful rewards, but a promotion structure with a path to the top must be clear to all so that those who are rightly ambitious can see where they are going. Financial rewards are also important or the lure of larger pay packets in the private sector, at least in a good economic climate, may still prove too strong. Whether it is tied to performance in post (a concept that is difficult to implement fairly) or to the post itself is immaterial. The pay packet must reflect responsibility; those with much responsibility must earn substantially more than those without. This is of course a quick way to redistribute the talent from the private offices and secretariat branches to where the real work is done. It should ensure that those who reach the top have a good deal of experience in the real world of procurement rather than in theory and Mickey Mouse accounting, and thereby guarantee a much improved effectiveness at the top.

Longer tenures, more specialist experience and higher pay for major responsibility may be possible without too much change for civil servants and scientists, where the rank structure is less rigid, than for the military. Scientists in particular are far less deferential to their bosses than are military men. It is the military who will find it hardest to change. To be fair, it has changed to some degree – more officers are serving longer in individual posts and are increasingly filling a series of related posts; but there is still a long way to go. What is needed is a move away from the traditional command-based promotion policy to a much more flexible one which ensures that MOD posts are filled by those who have the knowledge and expertise to succeed in the very different environment of Whitehall as compared with the field. Why do we continue to specify that for almost every job in MOD at full colonel level or above, command of a regiment is an essential prerequisite? This is irrelevant. Of course, most of the best starters will have commanded a regiment but it should not be a *sine qua non*.

Longer tenures will also cause difficulties for the military without a change of policy. We must have some sort of specialisation at an earlier age instead of attempting to fit huge numbers with the wide experience necessary for filling the post of Chief of the General Staff. We should be more honest with more officers at an earlier stage without totally destroying the chances of the late developer. Provided there is a clear promotion route to a high rank within a particular specialisation, that should be satisfactory. If it is seen that specialisation, for example in equipment procurement, can lead to 3- or 4-star ranks, there should be no shortage of takers.

One further step would simplify matters even more. Why do we still insist on retiring officers at the age of 55 if they are below the rank of lieutenant general? This is an age at which officers have a wealth of experience and can contribute enormously, yet we retire them. The Army used to guarantee a career to 55 but does no no longer. Surely this barrier is now artificial and a grave disadvantage? Remove it and allow selected officers of all ranks (maybe the number would be small) to continue beyond the age of 55, and match the civil servants experience for experience.

The expertise argument must be extended to the scientists. They join to do research, not to become managers. The key scientific post is what used to be known as the superintendent: the day-to-day direction and supervision of research teams. This person must be a specialist (although this could be in a relatively wide area), not a generalist. They must not be bogged down with paperwork and 'management'. According to our underlying assumptions, much of the bureaucracy could be reduced, but the management load should be taken on either by a non-scientist or by a scientist with the necessary character who is hungry for a change. The superintendent, just like the project manager, must be the responsible person with the necessary authority to direct the research the customer requires. Just like the project manager, he or she must be paid properly, be able to see a clear scientific promotion path and be rewarded, if successful, with promotion in post. This would replace the current situation in which the research teams are professional, the scientific managers amateur, and direction and supervision of the research teams largely non-existent.

Too many civil servants, and a surprising number of military officers, use long meaningless statements or delicate embroideries of the truth, for several reasons. One of the most frequent reasons is to cover up for lack of knowledge. Those with knowledge and expertise have no need to obfuscate the truth, and I would hope that the changes outlined above would help to eliminate this unsavoury practice. It is deeply ingrained, though, and will take some time to disappear even with a will. Its disappearance would certainly improve efficiency and reduce amateurism.

In summary, there is an urgent need to introduce professionalism. While clear accountability and the integration of both responsibility and full authority in one person will bring about a major change, other innovations are necessary. Longer tenures in post, less movement between unrelated areas and adequate financial rewards must all be brought in, not only for the civil servants but for the military and scientists as well. The artificial military age ceiling of 55 needs abolishing so that expertise and experience are not lost at a crucial point. All this is perfectly possible; it will, however, need a major change of attitude at the top.

CHAPTER THIRTEEN

Effective Decision-Making

Whatever was required to be done, the Circumlocution Office
was beforehand with all the public departments
in the art of perceiving – HOW NOT TO DO IT.
CHARLES DICKENS, LITTLE DORRIT

One of the issues which unites many – perhaps most – people in MOD, as we have seen in Chapter Ten, is the overdependence on committees. The introduction of proper accountability together with the elimination of the ineffective and over-frequent scrutiny process along the lines suggested earlier would transform 'committee culture'. There would still be a role for the committee but it would be a much smaller, purely advisory one. The chairman, as the accountable officer, would be able to make the final decision whatever the view of committee members. There is a danger that his mind may be made up before the meeting and that he will hear only what he wants to hear. However, proper accountability which ensures that the chairman is solely responsible for that decision should make the competent man genuinely keen to extract the most from a committee.

There will inevitably be fewer committees and less frequent meetings for many of them, but not necessarily for all. Decisions will not need to await a meeting nor will meetings have to be convened in a hurry, with key people absent, to meet a decision deadline. The chairman or accountable official can take such decisions without committee help, drawing separate advice from individuals if they need to. Committees will therefore spend much less time on detailed decision-making, which will be done more and more out of committee. Does this mean there will be no real need for them? No, for I believe that the committee has a vital role to play in debating and co-ordinating policy across many areas. It is a scandal that some committees (such as the Equipment Approvals Committee when it was first set up) do not even refer to policy in its terms of reference, and that most committees fail to address it adequately even if it is part of their job. It is of course much easier to debate points of detail than to arrive at an agreed position on policy. And I mean hard policy: generalities and hot air do not constitute hard policy.

Committees are not the only advisory answer. They are time-consuming and largely inflexible. While there is much, often far too much, consultation at low level, there is astonishingly little at higher levels. Senior officers and officials are surprisingly loath to get out of their offices and discuss a burning issue with their peers. Lack of time is currently used as a common excuse, but the reduction in committee work would give people that time. More importantly, increased professionalism, as proposed in the last chapter, will enable senior individuals to discuss knowledgeably without the need for lengthy prior briefing and without feeling that they are being 'bounced' by a colleague making an informal visit.

An increase in knowledge, relevant experience and expertise, together with more time provided by less committee work and more discussion of proper policy will make senior officers and officials much more effective. Who knows? Individuals might conceivably begin to earn their salaries. They will, however, have to be ruthless with their private offices, secretariats and other supporting staff, not just in terms of reducing them but by ensuring that diaries largely emptied of committee meetings are not then filled up unnecessarily with other unproductive chores. As Alan Clark complained: 'They load my In-Tray with papers of widely varying importance and density, stacked haphazardly – the oldest, corniest trick in the Civil Service.'[1] If senior officers and officials are professionals they will be able to arrange their priorities correctly and see to it that their staff keep to clear guidelines reflecting those priorities. They will be accountable and they will no longer be able to duck the difficult decisions.

On what basis, besides knowledge, experience and expertise, will they make these decisions? After all, decisions should not be made solely on the basis of subjective judgement, of 'stomach-feel' as the Americans might say, or because 'that it is the way we have always done it'. There must be a firm objective base to important decisions. At the lower levels, this should not be a real problem. The question as to whether we should use this component or that can be answered readily by gathering the facts on the two and comparing like with like. At the higher levels, such an objective base is missing.

We must start with overall concepts. We urgently need agreed 'purple' concepts for tri-Service and single-Service operations. These have been pursued ever since Heseltine introduced further 'purple-isation' in 1985, but we have continually failed to come up with anything useful. What successful business operates without an agreed corporate plan covering its core operations? Concepts are fundamental to our future and we really must stop shilly-shallying and grasp the admittedly very vicious nettle. Grasped firmly, the pain will be much less; brushed against, and the nettle could destroy many people.

Grasping firmly means placing it at the top of top people's agendas. Work must not be watered down by those anxious to defend empires; if necessary they must be bypassed. This suggests that, at least temporarily, a 4-star general with 3-star support, working directly to the Chief of Defence Staff and ministers, should be given the job. He must have the necessary clout to hold off the single-service Chiefs of Staff who in the past have been wicked indeed in blocking progress (although I do have considerable sympathy with them, seeing that what has been put up has been incompetent rubbish written by well-meaning amateurs). Once written and agreed, the post of concepts chief can be downgraded a level or two.

Flowing from this 'purple' concept, which must be fairly detailed, the single-Service concepts can easily be written and agreed. From the single-Service and multi-Service concepts, doctrine can be written and agreed in the 'purple' concepts forum. Again, no amateurism should be allowed in these teams.

The directorates or divisions which have the responsibility for determining concepts and doctrine need, as I have argued earlier, to be placed within the equipment world, although many will disagree. The overriding reason is that concepts and doctrine have to be available in time for the accountable equipment person to deliver; if placed outside the equipment world, the long lead time of equipment decisions will be understood imperfectly and concepts and doctrine for the correct future time scales will not be available. Moreover they will need to draw on operational analysis, which for obvious reasons must remain within the equipment world.

Operational analysis is extremely valuable if carried out with a clear understanding of its limitations. As has been argued earlier on, very high-level analysis is largely a waste of time because of the myriad of variables, but lower-level analysis is most useful, particularly if due attention is given to input data, assumptions and sensitivity analysis. Working hand-in-glove with proper military judgement it can produce a strong basis for future decisions. If advanced computer prototyping is introduced at a very early stage of research, the basis will be further improved. All this must remain within the equipment world as lead times are so enormous, even if they are reduced drastically through the many proposals already made.

We should now have a strong and fairly objective (nothing can be entirely objective when looking so far ahead) basis, but there is one further ingredient which needs adding. If we know what we want in terms of the requirement, how do we decide what should fill it? A national solution or an international project, the cheapest or perhaps the most effective option? Value for money? Yes, but what exactly does value for money mean? Currently it means the best value for the money spent in the short term. Too often it means the best value over the next three years or so in terms of what the budget can spare. It does not always mean the best value for the procurement costs. It certainly does not mean the best value over the whole life of the equipment. And it decidedly does not take into account British industry, which must survive if we are to have options in the future for gauging differing value for money.

To select the most sensible, a proper evaluation of the full (for example 30-year) value for money of each option is needed. This will be difficult but cannot be impossible. Proper Department of Trade and Industry input and industrial views must be taken into consideration, as well as the more detailed cost-effectiveness evaluation of the technical options.

In summary, effective equipment decision-making requires, in addition to the proposals in the previous two chapters, the following changes: fewer committees, acting in an advisory role to an accountable officer, agreeing or co-ordinating hard policy rather than matters of detail. This will give the new professionals more time to consult and make properly informed decisions. The concepts and doctrine holes must be filled urgently and a short-term appointment at 4-star level is needed to raise them above the level of petty empire defenders. Concepts and doctrine must march hand-in-hand with operational analysis and early prototyping. Equipment option decisions, using this basis, must be made on a long-term (30 year) comparison of value for money, taking into account the industrial factors over such a period.

CHAPTER FOURTEEN
Streamlining Procedures

Life is one long process of getting tired.
SAMUEL BUTLER, NOTEBOOKS

Once the right individuals have been made properly accountable with requisite power, ineffective before-the-event scrutiny removed and replaced with less frequent in-depth audit at or after the event; once a quantum leap in individuals' expertise, knowledge and experience has been ensured through longer tours with possible in-post promotion and more, but not narrow, specialisation; and once large numbers of consensus committee meetings have been removed, we are in a position to take a look at streamlining procedures and working practices. This is essential and the need has been acknowledged both within and without MOD, both unofficially and officially.

Let us start with management which needs considerable improvement. If middle management becomes the key and higher management supports only where necessary and instead concentrates on wider policy, the need for so many layers of management disappears. This does not mean adopting matrix or flat structures but a flatter hierarchical structure where span and depth are in balance. Without the need to poke into day-to-day management, those above the assistant director or project manager level could cope not only with greater span but with greater depth. There is no need for a hierarchy of directors, directors general and controllers under the Chief of Defence Procurement, or of directors, assistant chiefs, deputy chiefs and vice-chief under the Chief of the Defence Staff. At least one if not two of these layers could be removed. The remaining individuals will only be able to cope if they leave the real job to the assistant directors, except where higher-level action is required. This does not mean they can slide out of touch, but they must remain in touch with the most important bones only. They will be providing guidance, not close direction, and guidance solely when needed. Only when high-level action is needed, which should be less frequent than at the moment, will higher management need to involve itself in anything more. The mania for detail 'in case it crops up in discussion' has to be resisted. And it can best be resisted by making the assistant director responsible for placing the facts before senior MOD committees.

Assistant directors should present their projects or submissions themselves, for example to the Equipment Approvals Committee, and should not waste huge amounts of time in extensive briefing of higher management to do so less expertly. The audit findings can also be presented by that level. The Committee can still remain small and can still reach decisions behind closed doors, but those decisions would be based on the facts presented by experts.

I have already proposed that return to the Equipment Approvals Committee must be infrequent – perhaps a minimum of three times over the whole period from the start of pre-feasibility to the end of full development. The Committee must not fragment its decisions at those points and must, if necessary, spend more time at each decision point rather than ducking certain decisions and directing that they be referred back in a year or so. The Committee has more than once expressed opposition to its heavy workload. Fewer submissions and less or no fragmentation of those decisions will give them much more time to concentrate for longer and in greater depth on those submissions that are made. If the Committee does its job in a professional way, any delay to the decision at this point will be the fault of the assistant director (either through a weakness in presentation or a flaw in the proposal) and not the result of unnecessary bureaucratic wavering. With the reduction in day-to-day management, they will be able to devote time to considering and agreeing equipment policy – an area which does not get any consideration at the moment, except in small, specific blocks taken out of context. This should lead to a major improvement in consistency both of the overall programme and of individual decisions; it will also ensure much better knowledge at the top.

While high-level committees will probably need to remain consensus committees, those chaired at director level and below must be chaired by an individual with the authority and responsibility to resolve the problem as acknowledged within MOD in the Macdonald Report on Working Practices in 1991. This must apply to the dossier working groups, where the dossier chairman currently has no real power at all. Indeed the dossier, which has many strengths, must be re-examined to eliminate some significant weaknesses. The need for consensus from a large body of people at the working level has to go, and so does the gap between the three-page 'fast track submission' (which regrettably often gets puffed up way beyond that simple-sounding title) and the whole caboodle. Earlier proposals should enable these weaknesses to be eliminated, particularly if the Operational Requirements branch head and the project manager are merged into one fully accountable post. The latter would chair the dossier working group, if indeed such a group is still necessary, and take advice on finance, contracts, operational analysis, other scientific studies and in-service repair and maintenance. Others, whether within or without the dossier working group, would have no power of veto or delay.

I have said that higher management must support the key middle managers and not direct them in day-to-day management and decisions. Guidance is the keyword and 'guidelines' must replace 'instructions'. Guidelines will be written for guidance, not for slavish obedience as happens at the moment. 'Instructions' have become mindless dogma which is a very real bane. Dogma must be eradicated for it presupposes that there is only one way of resolving an issue; there are, in reality, always several options for doing so and it is up to the accountable middle manager to pick the best, using the 'guidelines' as no more than one more aid to decision-making.

Rustication remains a real problem in the equipment world. It is inefficient enough having to gather numbers of people for a meeting at one of the many Defence Research Agency establishments or for them to visit London, but research is probably best done away from the hurly-burly of London politics. More serious is the establishment of the Army Doctrine Directorate at Upavon in Wiltshire and the move of the Procurement Executive to Abbey Wood. Both need day-to-day contact with many colleagues in London if they are to avoid ivory tower status. The Army Doctrine Directorate must move to Whitehall where daily face-to-face contact with the concepts and Operational Requirements teams is possible. Forget what the IT kings tell you: personal discussion is necessary.

As for the Procurement Executive, it needs to be in London for the same reasons, but also because London has the best transport links with the British defence industry. I can see that this reversal of the stated rustication policy – first for financial reasons, then for management reasons, never for MOD-wide effectiveness reasons – may well fall into the 'politically unacceptable' basket. After the merger of project manager and Operational Requirements branch head and that of some of their seniors, the remaining slimmer Procurement Executive can ply its professional agency activities from Abbey Wood; at least until the inefficiency caused by its location becomes obvious to everybody. The key issue is that those accountable for procurement decisions are in London and as close to Whitehall as possible. The only sensible alternative is to move MOD lock, stock and barrel to the Upavon–Bristol area and leave ministers to do the travelling. A non-starter?

There is currently an obsession with output. This is quite justified, provided this obsession is with useful output. It is difficult to measure but the sleuths are on the trail; hundreds of them. They need data by the barrow-load and they mean to get it. Numbers of this, figures for that, measures of the other – all without a clear plan. Wellington apparently had a similar problem with Whitehall when he was fighting the Peninsular War. The IT gurus make it worse. Of course we can collect, collate, manipulate, massage, process and display – all without thought of the useful end result. We obviously need data but let us collect only what is strictly necessary. Much of the data collected, on tasking and worksheets, about time spent on this and money spent on the other will be of no interest if an accountable middle manager is allowed to run his own empire; it will be small enough for him to know exactly who is doing what and why. Higher management must resist the urge to collect data just to mess around with day-to-day management or to sit upon.

Private offices must be reduced both in quantity and quality of staff. I am not suggesting that senior officials employ idiots, but they need people who are efficient at low-grade administration, arranging visits, diary, cars and travel; they do not need a barrier of high-quality Bernards preventing direct exposure of the Great Man to the world. With the disengagement from day-to-day management and reduction of routine committee work, they should have more time to deal directly with those under them on essentials such as policy or major difficulties in a project. They must keep their door open and forbid their outer office to hinder those trying to see them or to fill their diary with nice but unnecessary visits. They must know what is going on if they are to support, not direct, their key middle managers, and they will only find this out if they talk to them and not get second-hand versions filtered through their outer office. Managers must know that they can talk to them and seek guidance without the feeling that it is a black mark if they own up to a problem. Approachability is an essential quality and must be instituted. The 'five-minute chat' at all levels, as acknowledged in the recent Working Practices Study,[1] is far more valuable than any number of written briefs, however big and fat.

The big, fat brief may have to be retained for a few top-level international meetings where a small delegation is essential for a number of reasons, not least cost. Nevertheless, if the delegates are knowledgeable and expert, they do not need the Janet and John approach; all that they require are copies of minutes, papers to be discussed and key study findings relevant to them. They should know the rest, and if they don't they are showing themselves to be incompetent. While delegations should be small, they do not have to be composed inflexibly; they should be selected to match the key agenda items and may often include much lower-level experts to deal with the facts of the meeting. Continuity must, however, be provided and this should be vested in the head of delegation. 'Notetakers' are not required: each expert can do this vital chore on their own subject, the head of delegation the rest. And the latter must be a working head, not a figurehead without the figure-work.

Apart from these cases, big, fat briefs are out. Written briefs should be reduced and, when necessary, provided in the form of a one-side list of key points. Long background ramblings and listings of perfectly obvious implications should be unnecessary. The 'five-minute chat', the verbal brief and the short list of key points should be the normal options; formal written briefing very much the exception.

The electronic office is still light years away in the MOD procurement world. Until we are all on one electronic system, it will remain so. CHOTS is not what the systems area needs and, whether or not MOD ditches it, it should figure in the equipment world no longer than it takes to replace it. The replacement system must be common with the Procurement Executive (from all accounts DAWN might fill the bill) and must also be extended to the Defence Research Agency, the concepts and doctrine branches and users in the field. It surely cannot be beyond the bounds of possibility to get this right.

Security classification is another real irritant. Proper security is essential, even with the demise of the Warsaw Pact. There is, however, no penalty for overclassifying, lots for underclassifying. It is therefore easy for the sloppy-minded to slap 'SECRET' on a complete document rather than to identify those statements or figures that are actually classified. The height of absurdity was reached in a report on what was planned as a visit to an international armament exhibition in China. When the exhibition was cancelled at a late stage, it became a report on a visit to the Museum of the Long March and the weapons in use all those years ago. Unbelievably it was classified, and classified not just 'CONFIDENTIAL' or 'SECRET', but even higher. It was farcical but all too common. I took up this issue of overclassification in my last year of service and produced detailed arguments as to why each report was overclassified and where. All I got were defensive smoke screens. Does this overclassification matter? It does! Apart from devaluing the whole business of security ('That security breach doesn't matter, it wasn't really classified!'), it takes time and effort. And once the classification goes above 'SECRET', special handling procedures have to be used which are very time-consuming. Some will argue that it is too difficult to classify accurately and quicker to overclassify. It may be for the originator but not for everyone else. In the MLRS 3 project, when we found difficulties in exchanging classified data quickly between nations, the cold look at what really needed to be classified 'SECRET' or 'CONFIDENTIAL' led to the vast majority being declassified, leaving only a few protected key figures and statements. There was no reduction in security as a result. The onus must be on the originator to classify particular figures or statements rather than whole documents. This could revolutionise security classification and reduce enormously the effort currently involved.

In all these changes, the theme is a substitution of form for substance, and of procedures that put a meaningless 'tick in the box' with procedures that work effectively. It should streamline everything – reduce time scales, bring clear accountability at all levels, leave decisions in the hands of experts, eliminate meaningless data collection, reduce unnecessary, if well-meaning, interference by non-experts, decrease the very heavy briefing load significantly – and leave everyone with much more time and energy to concentrate on the important issues. One example I have mentioned before would be to leave the detail of the long-term costings of years five to ten and concentrate on getting the first five years right.

MOD has been in continuous and considerable change for the best part of a decade. There is much more to come. All this markedly reduces useful output; in the Procurement Executive for example the reorganisation, move to Abbey Wood and introduction of new IT could reduce output by 50 per cent over two years. We need to put a stop to such change, but before we do so we must get it right and then accept the position for the next decade or more. But getting it right takes time and clear thought from the top down. Change needs managing. To date it has not been managed and morale has fallen. Future management must be improved. If this happens on the above lines and if everyone is kept fully informed, the next few years need not be too painful. At least my proposals should make things much more efficient and reduce the paperwork drastically. Can pigs fly? No, but if we change the pigs to eagles, they will fly of their own accord.

CHAPTER FIFTEEN

Technical Partnerships

*Government and co-operation are in all things the laws
of life; anarchy and competition the laws of death.*
JOHN RUSKIN, UNTO THIS LAST

Like most marital partners in strife, MOD and industry are each blaming the other for the antagonistic way they have been facing one another since the honeymoon days of 'cost plus', particularly whenever finance and contractual issues are uppermost. Like most marital partners, each is right – and each is wrong. To carry the analogy further, one partner is outraged because he has found the other blowing the house-keeping money on covert binges while asking for more; the other partner is furious because of the first's overreaction and the imposition of tight, dogmatic controls which are not open to discussion on commonsense grounds. Damage on both sides.

Creating a harmonious, effective partnership between MOD and industry, given the recent history, will be difficult but is essential for the future welfare of both. Without the major changes proposed in the last four chapters it is likely to prove impossible, but let us assume that the changes are implemented: That a strong, competent Project Manager, merged with the Operational Requirements branch head, with the right knowledge, expertise and experience, supported but not closely managed by those above him, has the authority to match his responsibility, the ability to make almost all decisions throughout development without reference either upwards or sideways unless he wishes and is not required to spend any significant part of his time on briefing, submissions, or other bureaucratic paperwork; restricted only by infrequent in-depth audits. With these changes, the move to a harmonious, effective partnership with industry is much easier. However, further change is still necessary, largely in outlook and attitude.

The first issue is trust. A weak person, hemmed in by threatening higher management, will never be able to trust a strong equal if that equal has different aims. A strong, independent person, however, will do so if he can. This is not to say he should be gullible, but he must develop a sense of when he can leave well alone and when he cannot. This sense is not an inbred characteristic but comes with knowledge and experience. A strong, independent project manager will gain industry's respect, as has been amply demonstrated on the few occasions when such a person has operated under today's restrictive guidelines. Gaining the other's respect is a major step forward.

But respect alone is insufficient. He must have strong clout which he can use when he needs to, and this clout must be recognised in advance by the other side. It must not rely solely on terms of contract as these are often difficult to make absolute enough to stand up in a court of law when both sides may be represented by very able lawyers. MOD must be able to blacklist firms which have forfeited trust. This list could contain several gradations of pain, from a weighting against competitive bids through a time ban on placing contracts with that firm or part of it to a full blacking of that firm for all contracts in the future, limited or not by a period of time. This blacklist should be publicised. While there may well be legal difficulties with doing so, I believe that the threat, together with very limited use, should be a sufficient deterrent. If it threatens the future of the company, higher management is bound to take a closer interest in certain projects. This in itself would eliminate two of the greatest failings in the British defence industry: an aloof, time-myopic higher management, and a weak middle management that is timid about carrying bad news up the chain. If it results in more engineers and fewer accountants on the board, so much the better.

The changes I proposed for MOD are far-reaching, but they must be echoed in industry. There is no reason, though, why MOD should not lead in the expectation that industry will follow. In view of stronger, more independent and expert project managers with real ability to hurt, they will have to. Some firms have already gone as far as they need, but the majority still lag behind badly and some are just plain incompetent. This is not the place, nor am I the man, to propose measures for reorganising industry's organisation, procedures and manning, but the faults noted in Chapter Seven must be eliminated. Unless this is done soon, many more firms will go to the wall. There is no point in asking MOD to buy British if that is a bad option.

'Buying British' is of course a major bone of contention. Sir Peter Levene's competitive revolution gave no quarter: best value for money would win the day, whether it was a bid from a British firm or a foreign one. No national favours were on offer. This was a major source of strength, but it cannot be a long-term strategy without some modification. It has to take account, amongst other things, of the huge size of production runs in the United States and French government support of its industry.

The major weakness with this hard-nosed strategy is the difficulty of determining value for money. At the beginning this was too often associated with the lowest bid; later it improved but was still a short-term view. It needs to be made on a long-term basis including such issues as the survival of British industry and its ability to make competitive bids in the future. Of course this is difficult. There can be no absolutes in the long term, which means the whole life of the project. If there are no absolutes, then MOD can operate a competition how it wishes and be public about it without fear of legal challenge.

My view is that we should replace a policy which effectively places the onus on British companies to show that they are better than the foreign opposition over a relatively short period with one that places the onus on the foreign opposition to show that over a full project life they are better value for money than the British bid. This is still basically a fair competition, far fairer in fact than international competitions held in other countries. It would certainly give British firms encouragement and incentive. By winning more MOD competitions, they would be in a better position to win more foreign competitions as well. This in turn would make them even more competitive in Britain itself.

None of this is likely to undermine such competitions in the eyes of foreign competitors; what does is a last-minute turnaround when ministers realise that jobs will be lost in a marginal constituency if a foreign bid wins. Such political factors will not go away, but if they are considered before an international competition is launched the damage will not occur at a later stage. That this gives a built-in advantage to a particular British firm is not that significant if, as I have suggested, a strong, independent project manager has the power to inflict substantial damage on the firm if it does not come up with the goods at a reasonable price.

We can go further. To ensure the survival of more than one British firm in any one area, a system of preferred contractor for each project could be operated, only to be overturned if the rival bid is clearly far superior. This will be difficult to implement fairly in some areas, but a similar policy is used in other countries to the benefit of both government and industry; it is therefore possible to operate and Britain would be stronger for it. It should not be forgotten that for every £1bn lost to foreign competition some 40,000 defence jobs are at stake. Foreigners will pledge 'off-sets' but it is clear that 'off-sets' do not work, neither in quantity nor in the quality of work which eventually comes back to the United Kingdom in other projects. There is, of course, some added risk to MOD here, but I do not believe it to be large. Moreover, higher risk in a much more cost-effective procurement policy is better and probably cheaper than lower risk in an ineffective one.

To summarise, a strong, independent MOD project manager, with a stick big enough to inflict serious damage but used only very sparingly, operating a procurement policy less hostile to British firms, will be of enormous benefit to the British defence industry. To take advantage, defence industrial managers will have to change their organisation, procedures and attitudes. They must do so.

It is not just the MOD–industry partnership which needs attending to. The MOD–Defence Research Agency (DRA)–industry research partnership is also in need of improvement. The biggest single factor here is shortage of money, caused not only by top-heavy management and risk aversion but also by the refusal to provide an adequate sum in the first place. As argued earlier, research spending by MOD and by industry must increase drastically; in my opinion it should be doubled. MOD can easily afford this: a two per cent rise within the current overall defence budget would not be impossible to find, but with the changes I have proposed there will be plenty to spend on research. If industry doubts its ability to find another one or two per cent to double its research (not research and development) spend, I suggest it looks at management overheads and the publicity budget.

Current reorganisation in MOD in the wake of the Defence Costs Study should result in tighter control by the MOD customer of DRA activities and in fewer management personnel involved. Whether this will work without further changes is doubtful, and even if it does it would be wasteful. Bureaucracy needs to be limited and scientists must be employed primarily to do research or to supervise it, not to manage the resources. Unlike industry, MOD has a preferred research partner in the DRA. Regrettably, trust has not been established satisfactorily. It exists at the bottom in some areas and very patchily further up. But top management has consistently undermined the MOD customers' trust by concentrating on superficial indicators of performance rather than on the substance of quality of output. Timeliness is of course important but I would rather have quality late than substandard work on time. So, I suspect, would anyone who has to use the output rather than just talk about it.

The trick is to produce quality on time. This can only come about through much closer dialogue between the MOD customer and the research scientist supervisors who know what's what. Do away with the middleman and the dogmatic managers. Having decided their requirement, all the customer needs from the scientist is an estimate of man hours required to complete a job. It cannot be exact as research is not exact but the customers can shape their budget progressively through the year as one area overspends and another underspends; they need not worry the research scientist except in placing work. The scientist will still have the problem of providing the right staff effort but he could rely much more on buying in such effort or contracting out packages of work to industry.

This last point would allay to a large extent industry's suspicion of the DRA. They see MOD's precious research spending being given uncompetitively to the DRA with little or no useful work for industry to compete for. It is not quite as black as industry makes out, but this is the way they see it. And the DRA's much-trumpeted 'Pathfinder' programme, so mismanaged by the DRA at least in the first few years, has not been a help. The MOD customer should not be dependent on the DRA for agreement to let a contract to industry; he should do what he thinks right. Close dialogue with both the DRA and industry will help to ensure that the MOD customer chooses sensibly. There are weak areas and there are understaffed areas in the DRA; work put to industry in those areas would appear to be to everybody's advantage. More research spend is the key. Without it, it is difficult to envisage either the DRA or industry being satisfied with what they get. Double it.

The third and final technical partnership that needs consideration is that between the MOD Procurement Executive and the It specialists. The reorganisation within the Operational Requirements world to make a brigadier directly responsible to ACDS OR(Land) for all land systems IT, both operational and non-operational, is a good basis. But the action required is drastic. Within the equipment procurement world, it is vital that in the near future all important directorates, executives and agencies are on the same IT network. It would help if the non-equipment directorates were also on the same system, but this is not essential if they are all collocated in the Whitehall area. At the very least, the Operational Requirements staff, the Procurement Executive and the DRA must all interface electronically. It is highly desirable that concepts, doctrine and the key equipment staff amongst users in the field are also electronically compatible. Electronic links with industry must be possible.

CHOTS is clearly a non-starter for all this and should be abandoned right away. Whether either the Procurement Executive's DAWN or the DRA's IT system could act as the basis is not clear, but it is vital that one system is established in the near future to do what should have been obvious when current IT was being planned (or not planned as seems to be the case).

As for operational IT, the reorganisation in the Operational Requirements division should do the trick. However, the record to date is so poor that it will be crucial for the IT specialists to be brought firmly to heel and that requirements, not technical possibilities, lead the way. This will be breaking new ground and, if it takes hold, could revolutionise the whole defence IT world. But I do not underestimate the inertia which will oppose change. Whether a true partnership is the way to go is debatable, but it should be presented as such, even if it is in fact an iron dictatorship of the requirement in a velvet possibilities glove. A psychological approach might reap the reward of IT specialist co-operation in such a dictatorship.

Partnerships are seen as a good thing. Currently there is much talk about partnership with industry and other Departments of State but precious little action. Clearly a partnership is required between MOD and industry if both are to survive in a satisfactory form in the future. It is perfectly possible, but it requires far-reaching changes on both sides as discussed above. A research partnership between MOD, DRA and industry is more problematic as it is crucially dependent on more research funding. This must be found, for the very future of this country's defence effort is at stake. It could come from within present budgets – after all what is another one or two per cent? – but if the proposed changes are implemented, more money should be available, unless it is all raided by the Treasury. As for IT, there must be a dictatorship of the requirement, albeit presented in a velvet glove, and this must include a defence equipment-wide IT system. Without it, we remain amateurs.

CONCLUSION

A Blueprint for the Future

Progress, man's distinctive mark alone
ROBERT BROWNING, A DEATH IN THE DESERT

ACTION SUMMARY

Organisation
- Responsibility and authority given to single-Service Chiefs of Staff to deliver a capability in the field, including the provision of suitable and cost-effective equipment.
- For the Army, current MGO and ACDS OR(Land) posts to be amalgamated into one 3-star post directly responsible to CGS for all aspects of Army equipment procurement. Other Services likewise.
- MGO to have two deputies at major general/director general level with role of co-ordination, guidance and policy formulation only. No direction or day-to-day management.
- Project managers and Operational Requirements branch heads to be amalgamated and given both responsibility and authority. These posts to be rank-ranged from colonel/assistant director to brigadier/director. Similar posts for research, retitled as programme directors. They will be the engine room of a new single-Service Requirements Executive.
- A 4-star officer, reporting directly to CDS, to head a 'purple' concepts division. Downgraded to 2-star once satisfactory 'purple' concepts are endorsed.
- Single-Service concepts and doctrine directorates to be included in single-Service Requirements Executive.
- Small Procurement Agency to be formed from rump of current Procurement Executive to do routine common tasks of contract writing, financial bookkeeping and project milestone evaluation. No responsibility for scrutiny of requirement, specification or policy.

Accountability
- All posts of responsibility to have requisite authority to enable the holder to make decisions and carry them out without consensus from elsewhere. This includes financial authority.

159

- Current scrutiny to be discontinued and replaced by in-depth, infrequent audit.
- PUS to be responsible for audit at a few specific points in project history – once at the beginning of pre-feasibility, once at the start of the current Project Definition Phase 2, and once before production is started with no more than three, and preferably no, other points during development.
- Audit teams to be drawn from PUS's permanent team plus outside experts. Audits to last about a week but dependent on size and complexity of project. Findings to include significant issues only. Responsible for keeping and disseminating lessons learned, through central living document.
- Result of audit, plus programme director's assessment, to be presented by working-level experts to top equipment committee to consider in depth. Fewer submissions will allow more time for committee consideration of each project.
- Accountability to be based on substance, not form.

The Programme Director
- Formed from amalgamation of project manager and OR branch head. These key individuals to be carefully selected, given full powers with clear accountability, and supported, not directed, by higher management. No day-to-day scrutiny of actions from outside.
- Expertise, knowledge and experience to be drastically improved, partly through better training but mainly through longer terms (up to ten years), less movement between very different areas, and specialisation in related areas.
- Promotion in post for the successful. Posts rank-ranged from colonel equivalent/assistant director to brigadier equivalent/director.
- Pay for programme directors to reflect responsibilities; substantially more than in posts of equivalent rank without such responsibility. This should help to redistribute talent satisfactorily and give motivation for lower project staff.
- Route to the top, post programme director, to be clear to all.
- Early sack for the unsuccessful.
- Military promotion less dependent on command success; earlier specialisation; no mandatory requirement for retirement below 65.

Higher Management
- To act in support of programme directors and other key middle managers. No day-to-day direction or management. No scrutiny role.
- To establish top-level policy, particularly overall equipment policy; to co-ordinate and issue guidelines rather than instructions or dogma. 4- and 5-stars must earn their salary; no ducking of difficult issues. Leadership required – no inert figureheads.
- Retain hierarchical structure but flatter and more flexible. Remove one or two top-level layers.

- Reduce quality and quantity in private officers to remove the barrier to real workers seeking guidance; keep diaries free of trivia and attractive but inessential trips to maximise time for essentials; open-door approach rather than briefing and meeting culture; no 'big, fat briefs'; more informal discussion with peers
- Top-level international meetings to be attended by experts in support of one top person who must use experts to present or argue case. No automatic places apart from head of delegation who provides necessary continuity. Selection of experts dependent on the agenda – no 'trips for the boys'. Briefs can then be restricted to one-page list of key points and essential background papers for reference in discussion.
- Manage change positively; keep morale up by disseminating better and more truthful information.
- Bring continuous change culture to an end. But get it right first.

Committee Work
- Reduce number of committees and attendance at each drastically.
- Committees, except in one or two cases probably at highest policy-making level, to be advisory to chairman and not consensus forum. Chairman to have power to make decisions without consensus and without delay. Committee members to have no power of veto or delay.
- Committees to concentrate on policy, not detail or hot air.
- Dossier system for equipment submissions to highest equipment committee to be overhauled to reflect new accountability and individual powers.

Scientists, Research and OA
- Scientists to concentrate on research and supervision of research, not on management.
- Superintendent to become key scientist rank with full responsibility, authority and accountability to carry out research required by the customer. Superintendents work direct to the research programme manager in the Requirements Executive.
- MOD research funding to be doubled. Research work to be placed direct with industry where DRA weak or under-expertised. More DRA work to be placed by DRA with industry. Choice with MOD customer, not with DRA. But MOD priority to remain retention of high-class DRA with expertise in most areas.
- DRA to concentrate on quality of output.
- Industry to match extra MOD research funding pound for pound.
- OA to be recognised clearly as one tool amongst many in decision-making process. To be used hand-in-hand with military judgement. High-level OA to be discontinued. In all OA, emphasis to be given to a high level of effort on identifying input data and assumptions and on carrying out sensitivity analysis.

161

Rustication and Exchange of Data
- All key decision-making directorates to be collocated in Whitehall Area.
- Move of PE to Abbey Wood to be halted and site sold off. (If absolutely necessary, the much smaller Procurement Agency could lodge at Abbey Wood, but this would be very inefficient).
- Army doctrine directorate to move from Upavon to Whitehall.
- Increase travel budgets to realistic levels.
- Data collection to be minimised. Data on 'management objectives', 'output', etc. not to be collected. Where output is not clear, disband branch or directorate.
- Cease detailed costing of years five to ten of LTCs. Replace with rough outline of years six to twenty only.
- Ditch CHOTS for equipment world and replace with one IT system to serve the new Requirements Executive, the Procurement Agency, DRA, concepts and doctrine directorates, the logistic world and equipment users in the field, and interfacing with industry. To be in place within five years.
- All IT to be requirement led and not technology driven. IT staffs to use English and not gobbledegook.

Value for Money
- Decisions should be made on long-term (30 year+) rather than short-term value for money.
- In the long term, there are no absolutes, so OA, military judgement and industrial realities must all be an essential part of the decision. Prototyping must be extensively used, particularly in research and pre-feasibility stages.

Partnership with Industry
- Strong, independent, expert programme director must be given strong clout in form of a blacklist for very sparing use with industry.
- In return, 'buy foreign unless British is clearly best' policy must be reversed to 'buy British unless a foreign option is clearly superior'.
- Competition, both national and international, must be retained.
- Before competition is announced, all factors including the political (for example, employment in marginal constituents) must be considered. If one factor is to be non-negotiable, competition to be tailored or bypassed.
- Industry must be coerced into change, maybe through use of blacklist.
- Introduce into MOD policy an element of the preferred contractor in every area to retain possibility of future national competition. If abused, use blacklist. This must not be done inflexibly and should be used only where appropriate.

Savings
- Savings could be expected to be made in following areas:

- large percentage of the current scrutiny and financial accounting posts
- higher management by removing one or two layers
- Central Staff posts which will be redundant when responsibility for equipment is shifted to single-Service Chiefs of Staff
- in reducing PE to small agency
- in private offices, secretariats, plans and policy branches to reflect lesser day-to-day direction role of higher management and 'open door' policy
- Large financial savings will be made through shorter development time scales (between £400m and £600m annually) and larger, shorter and more certain production runs (perhaps greater than £400m annually).
- Less waste with fewer cancelled projects, less delay, less circular study.

Costs
- Double research spending – £500m per year.
- Higher pay for key, accountable programme directors.
- New IT.
- Short-term reorganisation costs.

NOTES

Chapter One
1 *Statement on the Defence Estimates 1996*, Cm 3223, HMSO, London (1996)
2 Taylor, Brian, 'Coming of Age: A Study of the Evolution of the Ministry of Defence Headquarters 1974–82', *Journal of the Royal United Services Institute for Defence Studies* 28(3), p.44 (September 1983).
3 *MOD SIP Industry Consultation Study*, March 1994.
4 *Collins English Dictionary and Thesaurus*, HarperCollins, Glasgow (1994).

Chapter Two
1 *Statement on the Defence Estimates 1994*, Cm 2550, HMSO, London (1994).
2 Clark, Alan, *Diaries*, p.291, Phoenix, London (1994).
3 Ashbrooke, Major A F B, 'Officer Career Structures – The Requirements of the Top Army Appointment', *British Army Review* 102, p.69 (December 1992).
4 *Ibid.*
5 Field Marshal Earl Haig, address on receiving the Honorary Freedom of the City of Canterbury, 10 October 1921.

Chapter Three
1 *'Yes, Prime Minister.' The Diaries of the Right Hon. James Hacker*, vol. I, p.14, BBC Books, London (1986).
2 *House of Lords Weekly Hansard*, No. 1575, 26 July to 28 July 1993.
3 *Focus. The House Journal of the Ministry of Defence*, p.1 (December 1994).
4 *The Times*, 20 October 1994.
5 'Mr Ian McDonald's evidence to the Scott Enquiry, Day 28', 6 October 1993, p.45.
6 *Ibid.*, p.44.
7 'Sir Robin Butler's evidence to the Scott Enquiry, Day 62', 9 February 1994, p.56.

8   Mather, Graham, 'Nothing to Fear, Sir Humphrey', *The Times*, 14 July 1994.
9   *Ibid*.

Chapter Four
1   Divine, David,*The Blunted Sword*, Hutchinson, London (1964).
2   Quade, E.S., *Analysis for Military Decisions* (1964).
3   Davis, P.K. and Blumenthal, D., *The Base of Sand: A White Paper on the State of Military Combat Modelling* (1991).
4   The first four figures have been taken from the statement of Defence Estimates 1994. The figure for Eurofighter procurement is my own very rough estimate, derived from the requirement of 250 aircraft at £40m each (newspaper estimates vary from £30m to £60m) with a £300m lump sum for development. This would seem on the modest side. The figures for the spend on computers is a rough estimate and, in broad terms, is likely to be about right: compare the US government spend of $25bn per year according to the *New York Times, Fax Digest*, 12 October 1994.
5   Figures taken from *Forward Look* (1994), Table 1.4.2.
6   Bagnall, Sarah, 'Welcome to the £700M House that Zantac built', *The Times*, 18 April 1995.

Chapter Five
1   Winston Churchill to the Secretary of State for the Colonies, October 1940.
2   The term 'Office of Management and Budget' has now been scrapped and its component parts absorbed into the Central Staffs. I retain it as a useful term for the central financial management organisation.
3   Hart, David, 'Not Enough Bang for our Bucks', *Spectator*, 6 February 1993.
4   *Preview*, No. 20 (January/February 1995).
5   Evans, Michael, 'MOD's Biggest Spender Moves into £254M base', *The Times*, 18 December 1995.
6   Snow, C P, *Corridors of Power*, p.65, Penguin, Harmondsworth (1966).

Chapter Six
1   White, David, 'After the Fighting, the Entrenchment', *Financial Times*, 18 March 1991.
2   Clark, Diaries, p.288
3   Divine, *The Blunted Sword*.

Chapter Seven
1   Quoted in MOD SIP Consultation Study, March 1994.
2   Address by John Weston, British Aerospace, to Brassey's Seminar 'The Defence Conundrum: the Economy, the Treasury, the Ministry of Defence, Security and

International Securities', December 1993.
3 *'Yes Prime Minister'*, vol.II, p.231, BBC Books, London (1987).
4 *Preview. The Journal of the MOD Procurement Executive*, p.1, February/March 1994.
5 *Ibid.*, p.15.
6 *MOD SIP Consultation Study* (see note 1).
7 Speech by John Major at King's College London, 15 February 1994.
8 Weston (see note 2).
9 Witt, Michael J., 'U.K. Study Slams Defense Policy', *US Defense News*, p.25, 30 May 1994.

Chapter Eight
1 *Preview*, p.15 (February/March 1994).
2 *Preview*, p.16 (June/July 1994).
3 *CHOTS News* (June 1994).
4 *MOD SIP Consultation Study*, March 1994.

Chapter Nine
1 I am particularly indebted to David Redman and Peter Blessington for raiding their archives and coming up with many examples.

Chapter Ten
1 House of Commons Defence Committee, *Eighth Report*, 29 September 1994.
2 Secretary of State's Written Evidence to the House of Commons Defence Committee, 29 September 1994.
3 *MOD Paperclips*, Special Issue No 3, p.3 (January 1994).
4 Interview with Sir Christopher France, *ibid.*, p.10.
5 *Preview*, No. 15, p.2 (February/March 1994).

Chapter Eleven
1 Taylor, 'Coming of Age', p.44.
2 Williamson, Nigel, 'Whitehall let costs "run out of control" at British Library', *The Times*, 15 May 1996.

Chapter Thirteen
1 Clark, *Diaries*, p.251.

Chapter Fourteen
1 *Focus*, No.69, p.5 (March 1995).